PRACTICAL STRATEGIES FOR
INDIVIDUAL
BEHAVIOUR
DIFFICULTIES

Second Edition

Geraldine Mitchell

David Fulton Publishers
London

David Fulton Publishers Ltd
414 Chiswick High Road, London W4 5TF

www.fultonpublishers.co.uk

First edition published in Great Britain by David Fulton Publishers
1997
This second edition published 2001
10 9 8 7 6 5 4 3

Note: The right of Geraldine Mitchell to be identified as the author of
this work has been asserted by her in accordance with the Copyright,
Designs and Patents Act 1988.

British Library Cataloguing in Publication Data
A catalogue record for this book is available from the British Library.

ISBN 1–85346–730–8

Typeset by FSH Limited, London
Printed in Great Britain

Contents

Preface

Behaviour difficulties can often be eliminated if an effective individual plan is introduced at the first sign of difficulty. This book hopes to help classroom teachers, Special Needs Coordinators and the pastoral staff of primary and secondary schools, to plan and record such interventions. It is written in the full understanding that teaching is a stressful job and that there is probably no more deskilling aspect of the job than a child with unpredictable and difficult behaviour. Because of this context, I have used a fairly simplistic and directive style. As the situation becomes more predictable and manageable, teachers will feel able to challenge many of the seeming assumptions and add creative interventions of their own.

I have used 'he' throughout to facilitate communication; the strategies are effective with both girls and boys. They can also be used to draw out the overly withdrawn and inhibited child.

Where I have used words to describe adults looking after children, such as 'parents' and 'carers', these are intended to be interchangeable and to include all groups engaged in this activity.

*Helping children
to learn skilful
emotional
expression*

Acknowledgements

I would like to thank the children I have worked with over the years. Their humour and courage in the face of sometimes intensely difficult circumstances have been an inspiration.

I would also like to thank the teachers who have carried out the programmes in their classrooms.

Finally, thanks to my daughter, Sacha, for her encouragement.

Links Between Emotional Development, Self-esteem and School Behaviour

- At first, the human babies have two reflex reactions: 'approach' and 'withdraw'. They move towards things they like and away from things they do not like.
- These two categories of emotional response eventually divide into 'angry' – 'happy' – 'frightened' – 'sad' – and will remain virtually reflex until about $2\frac{1}{2}$ years of age.
- Human babies need attention to survive. They cannot feed themselves like other species. A lack of sufficient attention from adults is frightening for children.
- Between $2\frac{1}{2}$ years of age and adolescence ideally children learn how to express their needs, emotional and physical, in ways that can be recognised within their specific environment. Different cultures, family attitudes and family skill at expressing emotions effectively, will affect the usefulness of what a child learns. What may be clearly understood at home may be incomprehensible to the world outside.
- The child whose emotions are misread or ignored will present differently at school to the child who has learnt accurate expression by seeing the efforts of those around him to interpret his needs.

Emotional development

- Children arrive at school with different levels of skill in the expression of their emotions and with different attention needs.
- Most are within broad average with a few being really good and a few needing a great deal of help to get it right.
- It is in the interest of the wider community to identify those children who have unskilful emotional expression or are attention-needy and help them into the broad average group.
- It is important to make sure attention from adults maintains the same level when the behaviour improves.
- Inclusion in society begins in school.

Behaviour in school

Self-esteem

- A good level of self-esteem is created by being individually known and valued by the group we exist within, i.e. family, school, work, friends.
- If an individual is unskilful in emotional expression it is very difficult, or impossible, for people to know him accurately enough in order to be able to give him a feeling of being valued.
- Unless children learn how to make themselves known they cannot develop a satisfactory level of self-esteem.
- Many research papers over many years find low self-esteem present amongst children with both behavioural and learning difficulties.
- Good autonomous decisions can be made by the child with good self-esteem. All learning and social interactions require good decisions.

How to raise self-esteem or Helping children make themselves individually known and valued as an individual

- Ask open-ended questions and listen to the answer.
- Let children hear that we have listened to them by feeding back their words.
- Make good eye contact with children and encourage them to do the same.
- Use his name positively.
- Remember the upsets and difficulties he deals with on a daily basis and make sure the child knows that you value the extra hardship or unfairness they deal with.
- Make it clear that you value all the children in your class, having taken the trouble to get to know them as individuals.
- Help unskilful children make themselves known to other children and adults so that they can be valued by them too.
- Help children to get it right because you care what happens to them.
- All the strategies in this book are intended to raise self-esteem.
  Difficult behaviour = unskilful emotional expression.

The teacher's context

- Teaching has been found to be in the top 2 per cent of stressful jobs.
- Behaviour difficulties are one of the most stressful aspects of the job.
- Teachers are used to being skilful at 'reading' children; it can be uncomfortable when this is really difficult.
- If it is unpredictable when the child will disrupt the class – the stress is the same as if he was doing it all day, everyday – even if it only happens once a fortnight.
- It is possible for the teacher to retrieve a proactive position where progress can be measured and an objective view can be maintained.

- Sometimes help is needed to get out of a situation where, as a teacher, you are being drawn into playing the other half of a dysfunctional behaviour. In order to lead the child forward to more skilful emotional expression we must remain skilful ourselves. This is not always easy.

- Step 1 – Observation and information gathering.
- Step 2 – Defining the problem.
- Step 3 – Planning the strategy.
- Step 4 – Carrying out the intervention.
- Step 5 – Evaluating success and re-defining remaining difficulties.
- Step 6 – Planning the new strategy.

The method

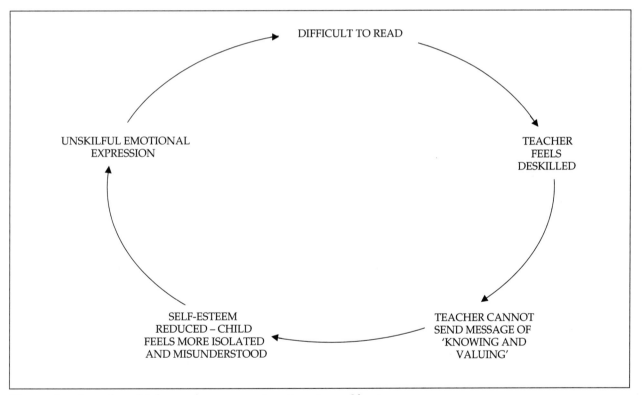

Figure 1   A cycle which needs overcoming to raise self-esteem

Observation and Information Gathering

To get a baseline of the current situation the teacher undertakes the following observation without informing the child.

In secondary school this needs to be collated by a year head or tutor set teacher. A blank timetable can be given to each teacher to fill in the appropriate slot (see Figure 1.1). The year head then puts these comments on the one-week-in-view sheet. The timetable can be adapted to include subjects, breaks, assemblies, etc. In the primary school the teacher keeps the sheet on their desk.

Observation should include anything the teacher feels should be there. Evidence of current interactive skill levels such as:

- good co-operation
- length of concentration
- signs of helpfulness
- cognitive success
- difficult sessions where the current problems are demonstrated.

At busy times the teacher may only be able to fill the space with a tick or a cross to indicate the success or otherwise of the session (see Figures 1.2 and 1.3).

Figure 1.2 is a copy of a weekly sheet of observations kept by a newly qualified teacher about a four-year-old. Years later when settled and happy with a foster family this child disclosed the horrific abuse he was subject to at this time. Figure 1.3 is a copy of a weekly sheet used on a successful programme with a 14-year-old boy who moved into the school's catchment area following a violent family break-up in which he had been stabbed by his father while protecting his mother. He was extremely volatile and aggressive. The dark patches on the figure have been coloured in red by his tutor set teacher as they were good comments.

Name_____ No. of goods _____ Target_____ Week ending _____

MONDAY	TUESDAY	WEDNESDAY	THURSDAY	FRIDAY
		BREAKTIME		
		LUNCHTIME		

Figure 1.1 Example of a weekly observation sheet

5

Name _____   No. of goods _____   Target _____   Week ending _____

	MONDAY	TUESDAY	WEDNESDAY	THURSDAY	FRIDAY
	Work sheets Read books PE – well-behaved	Pretty bad day – reluctant to work – except with one-to-one help from Sue	Worked well – 2 language sheets and read very well. Wasted after break – would not do anything	Good am – very excited. Worked well – in a good mood. P visited (Social worker)	Off all day
BREAKTIME	Exposed himself to Shane – Shane very upset. Work sheet half done. Three books read, enjoyed snap played – getting better. Alphabet work getting better, listened to tape	Tired	Very tired. Scratching again	Went to park, walked round school, coloured book and jigsaw. Did not want me to go	
LUNCHTIME	Bad language. Reluctant to do anything by himself, tired and fed up	✓	Read 1½ worksheets. 'Jigsaw'. Reluctant to work. Better on alphabet work – pleased with himself about it. Wanted to run round – wet day – in all play time	Worked well as part of yellow group – electricity experiment	
AFTERNOON PLAY	✓	✓	✓	✓	
STORY					

Figure 1.2 Weekly sheet of observations about four-year-old

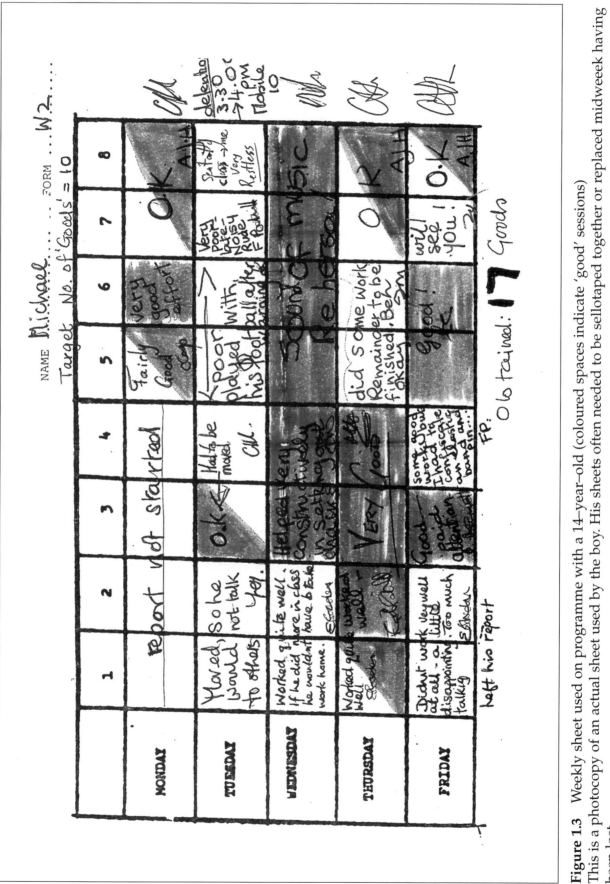

Figure 1.3 Weekly sheet used on programme with a 14–year–old (coloured spaces indicate 'good' sessions)
This is a photocopy of an actual sheet used by the boy. His sheets often needed to be sellotaped together or replaced midweek having been lost.

7

Record for the Code of Practice

Example

Initial concern

Pupil X arrived at this school two weeks ago. He appears tense and anxious. There have been several incidents of aggressive outbursts. In class he appears to be underachieving, appears to lack concentration and distracts others. There does not appear to be an obvious pattern to his difficulties.

Record academic evidence in the usual way.

Strategy

1. A two-week recorded observation will be carried out without the pupil's knowledge.
2. The pupil's parents to be invited to meet with teacher/pastoral staff to develop understanding of pupil's current situation. Has moved to this area due to family changes.
3. Record academic strategies in the usual way.

The reasons behind this method of observation

You may be anxious to get started on reducing the problem. It may feel like delaying to carry out an observation of this sort.

However, the two-week initial observation is probably the most important part of developing a successful programme that will eliminate the behaviour problem.

1. Teaching is a high stress job and nothing is more stressful about it than unpredictable behaviour.

> **Keypoint** – What a behaviour problem 'feels' like to the teacher is not always the same as what is actually happening.

Teachers I have worked with regularly note the findings of this observation method create unexpected results.

Keeping this type of record helps you objectively quantify and describe what is actually happening. It also helps you to map your progress.

2. This way of observing makes it possible to gain a sense of how the child's home life is affecting their day at school. It soon becomes clear for instance if bad days follow the child arriving upset in the mornings. Strategies for this are dealt with in Step 3.

   This pattern often also shows the child obviously enjoying school days when there have not been problems before school.

3. It is also possible to observe patterns in a child's week where certain days coincide with particular behaviours within the school. It is possible to clarify which sessions are regularly successful and which are not. This knowledge helps you to

understand the actual problem and direct your strategies to eliminate it.

4. Sometimes the findings highlight a whole-school or class issue that needs attention. A frequent example of this is the midday playtime.

5. It can also reveal the comforting information that some sessions are regularly successful. This is very helpful as there will be elements in that session that help you understand the child and plan the way forward.

6. If someone from an outside agency comes into your room to observe the child, while this can be useful, there are some problems with this.

    (a) The group dynamic changes as the ratio of adults to children is immediately halved. This method enables you to gather observations in the normal setting.

    (b) It is chance whether the difficult behaviour will be performed during the half hour the person is in the room. Assumptions made from such a snapshot may not be useful. What is more useful to be aware of is the whole weekly performance and the current level of success as a baseline to build on.

    (c) Planning the strategies you are going to carry out is a very personal activity for a teacher. If you have observed the problem objectively, analysed patterns yourself and planned a strategy you feel is practical for you to carry out, you are more likely to stick to it. It also means you can congratulate yourself when it succeeds!

       Sometimes programmes designed by other people for you are difficult to remain committed to.

7. The first statistic that will change when your programme is successful is the frequency of the behaviour not the intensity.

   This method of recording helps you monitor easily both the frequency and the intensity of difficulties. When you compare this to the frequency of good sessions you will be able to recognise immediately when the programme is working.

   Sometimes good programmes have been abandoned because the behaviour has occurred again, when actually it was already happening less often.

8. As your programme continues the weekly sheets form an administratively simple way of recording the programme; you can note on the sheets symbols to show you have applied various strategies at different times. These can be attached to the Code of Practice recording sheets.

9. I have known these sheets to be very useful if it becomes necessary to work with Social Services regarding Child Protection Issues. You can offer the social worker 'fly on the wall' records over a long period of time. The evidence you

present of days when the child was more upset than others may usefully coincide with information they already have.

10. This method also helps you remain objective. You count the 'goods' and if they have increased you can enjoy a sense of achievement.

11. If a sustained improvement suddenly deteriorates you are alerted that something has changed in the child's life. This change may not be at school.

12. It enables you to say confidently to a child: "While I don't like that behaviour and you must complete the sanction like any other child, I am very pleased that you haven't done that for three weeks. Do you remember when you used to do this every day?" The programme is for the long term.

Step 2

Defining the Problem

The classroom teacher, or tutor set teacher, with either the SENCO, year head or a colleague, examine the sheets resulting from the observation and discuss possible patterns. Count how many 'good' sessions there are each week and record this number on the sheet.

Some patterns you might find:

I   The child performs better when a teacher is present but gets into trouble when midday supervisors are in charge, or in any open-ended, less supervised situation.

II   The child copes well with the freedom of the playground but resists complying in the classroom.

III   (a) Child gets on well with adults one-to-one but finds peer group difficult.

      (b) Child withdraws to isolated position and has become an entrenched 'loner'.

IV   Certain days stand out as being regularly more difficult than others, or unpredictably some days are 'wiped out' from the start. Is it school-based activities that are different, or something at home?

      (a) Are there Child Protection Issues? Is there evidence of:

- sexualised behaviour?
- self harm?
- stealing?
- soiling?
- bruises?
- physical neglect?
- deep anxiety?
- distraught tantrums?

      (b) Does the class spend time in difficult areas on that day? This could be either acoustically difficult or the size of the groupings they are in on that day. Is there a change of teacher that is significant?

      (c) Do the opportunities presented on those days feed into the child's problem, i.e. mostly 'open-ended' or mostly 'on-task'?

(d) Does the child arrive upset and often late?

(e) Do certain visitors to family or other domestic changes coincide?

(f) Is the child reluctant to change for PE?

V   The child appears to be inappropriately tired and/or hungry.

VI   Lateness prevents peer group social contact before school.

VII A small insult or provocation from another child sets off an over-reaction in the child. This includes physical aggression.

VIII It seems the child cannot easily 'bring himself to a state of calm' once upset.

IX   (a) The child seems to resist becoming 'absorbed' in a task and seeks attention from adults and/or children at those times when 'absorption' is required.

(b) It seems that the child cannot work without one-to-one support from an adult.

X   There is a deterioration in behaviour after weekends or holidays.

XI   The child works well on very structured 'safe' work but does not respond well to open-ended creative work.

XII Child appears to find praise difficult to accept.

XIII Other patterns not mentioned here.

Strategies for each of these patterns appear in the next chapter. They are numbered as above, starting on page 18.

Record your definition of the problem for the Code of Practice

Defining the problem

List the descriptions that describe the problem – either from above or ones that you decide on yourself. Make sure these are objective.

Some examples of definitions of problems

1. *A Reception-aged child*
   - appears inappropriately tired
   - three days of the two-week observation seemed to have 'gone wrong' from the minute he arrived; he seems upset, angry, or depressed
   - 27 out of 40 sessions scored 'Good'
   - finds peer group relationships difficult can be excessively physically aggressive: six incidents over two-week period
   - appears to enjoy one-to-one time with adults
   - likes praise which is emotionally cool
   - stays on-task better in very structured sessions
   - break times often include incidents

2. *A Year 2 boy*
   - gets on well with adults one-to-one but finds peer group difficult
   - gets into trouble when midday supervisors are in charge, or in any open-ended, less supervised situations
   - some evidence of physical neglect: very dirty T-shirt and fingernails
   - finds peer group relationships difficult – can be excessively physically aggressive
   - works well on very structured 'safe' work

3. *A Year 4 boy*
   - often absent or late on Mondays
   - there is a deterioration after weekends and holidays
   - gets into trouble in less supervised situations
   - at times appears inappropriately tired and hungry
   - a small insult or provocation from another child sets off an over-reaction – this includes physical aggression
   - resists becoming 'absorbed' in classroom tasks
   - works well in structured sessions
   - relates warmly to adults in individual sessions

4. *A Year 7 girl*
   - certain days stand out as being regularly more difficult than others; school activities not different on these days
   - on these days displays deep anxiety, hurting herself by digging her pencil in her own hand
   - some episodes of stealing
   - arrives late
   - physical neglect
   - has withdrawn to an isolated position and became an entrenched loner
   - finds praise difficult to accept
   - relates well one-to-one with some adults
   - works well on other days
   - likes Art
   - resists absorption in task

5. *A Year 9 boy*
   - frequent absence
   - resists absorption in 'on-task' session
   - slight provocation produces an over-reaction
   - finds it hard to calm down after getting upset
   - can be very helpful to year head
   - taunts younger or less powerful peers

Which children need individual behaviour programmes?

Even in a perfect whole-school atmosphere there will always be children whose emotional needs are outside of broad average.

Outside-of-broad-average experiences produce outside-of-broad-average emotions. The child needs to convey emotional experiences few may identify with. The child is not surprisingly unskilful at this kind of emotional expression. It is harder for him to make himself known as an individual to be valued by the teacher.

The difficult behaviour we see at school is in my opinion the result of unskilful attempts to express emotions.

Figure 2.1 shows the curve of normal distribution. I would suggest that whole-school and whole-class initiatives should be designed to create a high level of self-esteem, good behaviour and effective learning for those within a very wide broad average group. Some children may be so emotionally skilled their performance is well above broad average and some may be below.

It is my feeling that those who fall below this genorously wide broad average are 'upset children', 'very upset children' and 'very very upset children'. The individual behaviour programme is to help them express this upset appropriately so that they may receive the value they deserve.

The strategies presented in this book hope to teach children the skills they need to include themselves in the broad average group. When they have achieved this level of inclusion, whole-school and whole-class initiatives should deliver the amount of support they need.

It is the nature of schools to be continually evolving towards a better model. You may be working in a school with very high quality support from a range of whole school initiatives.

These may include:

- high level of clarity and support from senior management;
- 'cover' managed efficiently with the least disruption;
- staff self-esteem very high due to feeling individually known and valued by senior management;
- self-esteem enhancing script adopted by all teachers throughout the school day, reaching 5–10 positive remarks for every one negative;
- positive rewards philosophy underpinning a fully enacted whole-school behaviour policy;
- achievement assemblies which recognise effort as well as achievement;
- midday playground time enriched with games and activities within a calm, well supervised framework;
- flourishing connections with parents and the wider community;
- effective circle time in every class;
- good handovers between classes of individual behaviour programmes;
- well organised interesting lessons.

More usually schools will be working towards some of these and achieving others.

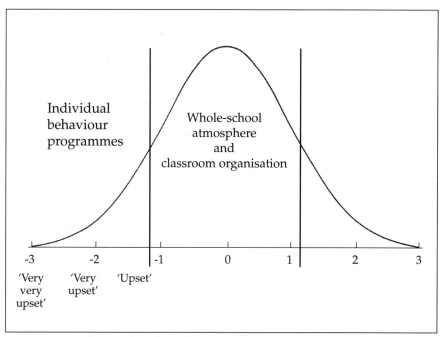

Figure 2.1 When individual behaviour programmes are needed

Planning the Strategy

Each of the patterns in Step 2 has a corresponding strategy in this section.

The aim is to increase the number of good sessions.

> **Keypoint** – Success will show first in a reduction of the frequency of incidents. The intensity will slowly reduce after that.

It is likely that during the observation period teachers will have already thought of some strategies to help the child improve his performance level. These should go ahead immediately if they are supportive to the child.

All normal school sanctions for rule breaking should apply throughout as for any other child in the school.

Sometimes teachers wonder if they have the time for strategies – Remember how much of your time these children control now!

A frequent question from teachers I have worked with is about which behaviours to target and how many strategies to put in place.

The intention is to view the child globally, to help them express themselves more skilfully and to increase the number of good sessions. A problem with targeting certain behaviours for elimination is that it may be shutting down an unskilful expression of an important communication.

Each of the patterns identified have a corresponding strategy in this section. Some of the best programmes I have seen teachers design have included a strategy for each of the patterns identified.

A child may be unaware they are on a 'programme' as such. The teacher may be using all of the following:

- Strategy IV – first thing in the morning if and when the child arrives upset.
- Strategy I – over the midday playtime for a couple of weeks till problem disappears.
- Strategy VII – a structured self-esteem enhancement programme to be delivered through classroom interaction, particularly highlighting successful sessions and decisions made by the child. A high ratio of positive remarks to negative of around 10:1.

- Strategy IX – during 'on-task' sessions in class
- Strategy X – The teacher may also be planning to meet with parents either at home or at school.

After six weeks, the teacher reviews the effect of these strategies. This review is discussed in Step 5.

The above programme is designed to help the child learn skills to cope better with the aspects of school they find difficult. This also confirms to the child that the teacher knows them as an individual and values them.

Look at the suggested strategies for each pattern in the list you have identified as part of the problem. Create your own programme to help the child.

Note for secondary schools

In secondary schools, subjects where children spend most time, i.e. Literacy and Numeracy, are best for in-class strategies.

The tutor set teacher and the year head can monitor the success of the programme across the curriculum and help the child with the organisation required (see Section XIII).

1. | **Keypoint** – What the behaviour 'feels' like to the teacher is not always what is happening. |

2. | **Keypoint** – All behaviour is communication. |

3. | **Keypoint** – Enhance the self-esteem necessary for skilful emotional expression and learning by helping a child feel known as an individual and valued. |

4. | **Keypoint** – All strategies should be explained when the child is calm. |

5. | **Keypoint** – A key need is to feel 'included'. He needs to experience that the reward for compliance to group boundaries is inclusion. |

6. | **Keypoint** – Every programme should demonstrate a wish to help the child become more skilful in the expression of his needs and emotions. |

Keypoints for all programmes

17

7. | **Keypoint** – Success will show first in a reduction of the frequency of incidents. The intensity will slowly reduce after that.

8. | **Keypoint** – Praise for expressing his needs becomes tangible if adults respond with understanding and kindness.

9. | **Keypoint** – If the problem is reducing, i.e. if there are more good sessions or less intense behaviour, continue with the strategy.

10. | **Keypoint** – The aim is for the child to have learnt new and successful emotional expression that he can generalise to all situations, particularly he should also be calm and express the problem.

11. | **Keypoint** – Congratulate yourself on changes that improve the situation!

What can I do about it?

In the following section the numbered strategies refer back to the list of patterns put forward in Step 2.

I Poor self-control in less supervised situations

This sometimes happens when there has been over-authoritarian and/or inconsistent control from adults in the child's life. It may be helpful to explore this with his carers, enabling them to find ways that they can help the child to make good decisions about controlling himself rather than maybe leaving unclear boundaries and then imposing heavy external control. Carers may not be able or willing to change.

Child's needs

The child needs help in small steps to internalise control of himself in a variety of settings and to feel proud of himself for learning to do so.
A letter home praising the child's efforts will be a very powerful reward.

Strategy

Dinner times

The following is a programme for dinner times but it can be adapted to suit other open situations. Sometimes supervision at dinner times varies in its effectiveness. If the child makes progress it is important that *all* adults let him leave behind his reputation.

1. Explain to the child in very few words that the playground must be 'safe' for all. That hurting people is not acceptable. He will be kept safe and so will others.
2. Explain that if he is not keeping it 'safe' you cannot let him go out.
3. Explain that you wish to help him 'earn back' going out.
4. If he sits quietly reading or drawing until the last five minutes of playtime he is allowed to go out.
5. A chart is kept by him and the teacher to record his progress. It may help younger children to colour in a chart showing each five minutes. It usually works, if done consistently, in about two weeks.
6. Each day that he does keep it 'safe', his time in the playground increases by five minutes.
7. If an incident occurs he goes back to the amount of time he was last successful for.
8. Letters praising his efforts should go home every time the time is increased. Older pupils may not find this rewarding unless it is as part of a full day programme. 'John has controlled himself well today and made good decisions.' 'John has achieved his lunchtime target today. We are very pleased with him. Well done John.' No letter is sent on days when it doesn't increase, and no recriminations. 'Try again tomorrow John, I'm sure you'll do better tomorrow.'

It may be the child complies too much at home. See also Section IX. It can also be that boundaries are very fluid at home. This can also happen when a child seems to have assumed an adult role with its carers and may have too much responsibility. It may be helpful to explore this with the carers. They may be unable or unwilling to change.

II Resists complying in class

Child's needs

The child needs to learn the pleasure of being guided by an interested consistent adult towards learning that is relevant to him. Praise in small steps for learning to trust the adult to set the agenda, along with praise for this from the head teacher and public praise in assemblies.

Strategy

See Section IX for use of timer to improve 'on-task' behaviour.

In the secondary context, this may be most effective and practical in English and/or maths, where more time is spent each week.

III Difficulties with peer relationships

This can occur for a number of reasons. For example, if a child spends most of his time relating to adults, he can become used to interactions being on his terms and find 'give and take' difficult. This can also result where intense sibling rivalry and/or dysfunction at home have created anxiety in this area.

Child's needs

The child needs to learn the social rules of child-with-child play and to experience the joy of successful cooperation. He also needs to make himself known to his peer group in a way that draws a feeling of being known and of value to himself.

Strategy

1. Choose a child in his teaching group who is well matched to the child's intellectual ability, not necessarily his attainment levels. This should be a child who would benefit reciprocally from the interaction once it becomes established. This could be as basic as 'they can make each other laugh' or 'they have an interest in common' or 'they see qualities to admire in each other'.

   In the secondary context, this can be monitored by the tutor set teacher and/or year head or SENCO. A standard report sheet can provide the feedback.

2. Whenever it is possible, put them together to work on a structured task, i.e. when others are in pairs or selected for particular tasks:
   - Paired work in PE.
   - Open-ended model-making.
   - Science experiments.
   - Survey work around school.
   - Design tasks.
   - Creative activities.
   - Classroom administrative tasks for pupils.

3. All the above tasks need conversation, sharing of ideas, listening to each other, respecting each other's views. Obviously, because the child is unskilful in these areas he will meet difficulties.

These are coaching points where the teacher can help them problem solve and move forward.

4. Praise should be given when something that was previously difficult, i.e. listening to the other child's ideas, is successfully done on another occasion.

5. Monitor the progress over half a term, using the sheets until the child can be seen generalising the skills he learns in this pair to the playground and other settings.

1. Are there Child Protection Issues? Follow Child Protection Procedures.
2. Arrange a hearing test to fully eliminate hearing as a factor.
3. Difficult areas on that day? See appropriate section, i.e. Section I where 'open-ended' situations are difficult, Section II where 'on-task' situations are difficult.
4. It may be that rows and/or lack of organisation at home are leaving the child feeling upset, angry and/or confused. This may also result in the child arriving late, and therefore missing peer group socialising time and whole-class start to the day. (See also Section VI for lateness.) The carers may not be able to change.

IV When some days are unpredictably 'wiped out' from the start

Child's needs

The child needs to find ways to 'de-role' from the disorder and remind himself that it is safe and peaceful at school, where he is understood and valued and that school is a place where children's needs are met. Even older children may have valid reasons for finding it difficult to get to school on time.

Strategy

This needs to be explained when he is not upset. Emphasis needs to be given that the strategy is to help the child.

The child is given time to sit quietly for 5–10 minutes on arrival with a chosen activity. For example, a tape with headphones, and/or reading a book, or colouring. The child is told that if he comes to school upset he should let his teacher/tutor know. This should be introduced with the goal of getting into the normal routine as soon as possible with praise for doing so. Consultation with carers regarding morning routine and explaining the importance of peer group time before school may also help the problem.

> **Keypoint** – Praise for expressing his needs becomes tangible if adults respond with understanding and kindness.

Many circumstances beyond the control even of older children can militate against success in this area. Younger children are dependent on adults completely for this part of their lives

V Inappropriate tiredness and/or hunger and/or inappropriately dressed

Child's needs

He needs to arrive at school appropriately dressed for the weather and rested so that he can relax, learn and play. He needs to be within broad average as regards cleanliness and personal hygiene so that his attempts to make friends are not unnecessarily difficult. Depending on his age and maturity he will need varying approaches to help him with this.

Strategy

1. Are there Child Protection Issues? If so, follow Child Protection Procedures.
2. If no Child Protection Issues apply, it may help to go through the weekly sheets with the carers to show them how the child's performance is being affected in school. It is important to give positive feedback to them if changes they make improve the situation for their child.
3. They may need reminding if the child appears tired again. This will be easier to do if you have praised the initial effort. The carers may not be able to change easily and may need regular meetings to monitor the situation.
4. He may be mature enough to work on cleanliness himself with a positive reward programme to give him praise for increasing the days he can arrive clean. Even older children can have circumstances beyond their control in the home that militate against success in this area.

VI Lateness prevents peer group social contact before school

The extent to which a child can arrive independently at school on time depends on age, maturity and circumstances.

With parental support, breakfast supplied and clean clothes made available, most secondary school pupils without learning difficulties can get to school on time. Some primary-aged pupils are also able to experience some independence in arriving on time. They may need convincing that pre-school socialising is worth getting up for.

However, without the above support and with the addition of difficult home circumstances, such as rows at night, chaotic organisation, younger siblings to look after and low status given to punctuality, a much older child could also find it difficult to arrive on time.

Very young children are at the mercy of their carers' punctuality.

Further, if learning difficulties, poor social skills or a bullying problem exist, motivation to attend can be affected. It may be the carers are not able or willing to change.

A working school is very hard to enter if you are late. The next step is truancy.

Child's needs

He needs to be at school in time to make satisfying contact with peers before the school day begins and know that he has heard everything from the tutor/teacher each day that everyone else has heard. He needs to feel welcome and understood for any difficulties, emotional or practical, that he may have had in getting himself there on time.

Strategy

Young children dependent on their carers
1. The child needs to know it is not his fault that he is late. He needs to see that you are glad that he has arrived and you understand if he is embarrassed by the lateness.
2. A meeting with carers to show them the weekly sheets and how lateness is affecting his performance on those days. Sometimes a discussion about the morning routine can be helpful to support the carers in planning it to meet the children's needs.
3. Carers sometimes say that the child makes them late by the difficult behaviour he demonstrates in the mornings. Some help with assertive strategies to dress the child and lead him firmly to school can be helpful. It can also be the case that the child is blamed unfairly to cover the carers' organisational lapses.
4. It is often helpful to put a follow-up meeting in the diary when all concerned know they will meet again to review progress on the weekly sheets. Obviously, it is appropriate to give praise to the carer who responds well and improves the punctuality. A gentle reminder may be necessary next time the child is late.
5. Persistent lateness undermines a child's ability to access his education and it may be that the Education Welfare Officer could give additional support within the home.

Older pupils

Whatever the circumstances at home it may be that a child can make his own plan with a teacher's help to improve the punctuality himself.

1. Find out from the child where the difficulties lie. Improve the circumstances that are within your power to change, i.e. bullying, being scared of one teacher, parents making unreasonable demands on his time.
2. Talk through with him strategies such as getting an alarm clock of his own, putting clothes out the night before, etc.
3. If he is telling you that rows at night prevent him sleeping, etc., he needs you to understand what he is battling with. He may have an ill parent or be sent to shops before school unreasonably.

    Whatever it is, you may not be able to change it but you *can* take it into account when you design the programme.
4. Let the child design the programme with you. Include elements such as:
    (a) He comes to say 'hello' to you, or his tutor set teacher, when he arrives and gets a star on a chart for being in time to socialise before school starts.
    (b) Some year heads have included a hot drink for the two or three pupils on this programme if they arrive early!
    (c) Agree a reward (see Section VIII) that is easy to provide regularly:
      • a letter home praising his efforts
      • housepoints (if the child values them)
      • public praise in assemblies.
    (d) If he's late – be glad he came and praise him for getting in. There should be no rewards or drinks, and normal school sanction for lateness applies. Help him to calm down and get into the appropriate lesson. Help him check he has the right PE equipment, books, etc., for the lessons he is going to that day.
5. Emphasise any improvement there has been and how many days since the last late attendance. Encourage him to put this behind him and be pleased if he's made the effort and gets in on time the next day.
6. When he suggests he could keep his score up without visiting you daily, let him try if you agree and monitor from a distance.

Support again if problem recurs.

VII Small things create over-reaction

There are many scenarios of pressure in and out of school that leave some children feeling very over-sensitive, to the point where any further slight is intolerable. Here are some examples, but see also Section VIII.

1. Abusive situations

These leave children feeling so needy they can be at 'breaking point'. One small thing can happen at school and all the feelings they cannot express elsewhere, that may have been bottled up, can suddenly pour out inappropriately. This is often called 'bizarre' behaviour as the observers cannot see how the outburst could be connected to anything they have seen happen. It is usually not 'bizarre' at all.

Usually one is seeing evidence that the child is under a lot more pressure in his life emotionally or physically than he is able to cope with. If the unreasonable pressure is not at school, it may be possible to discover where it is and help the child by facilitating changes. Adults can often be an advocate for a child to make changes it would be beyond the child's power to make on his own.

Child's needs
He needs to be in a daily situation which is at least averagely fair and safe. He may need caring adults to bring about changes for him that he cannot make himself.

Strategy
- If there are Child Protection Issues, follow the Child Protection Procedures.
- Where appropriate, work with parents to create change.
- Raise child's self-esteem.

2. Low self-esteem

Over-reaction can also be the outward sign of a child whose self-esteem is very low. This may be because he feels 'put down' a lot with unfairness and criticism. Any confirmation of his low value in others' eyes upsets him more because he already feels very bad.

Child's needs
The child needs his self-esteem raised by feeling known as an individual and valued.

Strategy
Specifically this means a structured attempt by the teacher to highlight real, positive traits in the child and good decisions that he already makes. These can be very small decisions at first, i.e. if he puts his coat on when its cold, the teacher says 'sensible boy, good

decision'. In the secondary school it could be arriving on time being noted by the tutor set teacher. The teacher continues to highlight all such small sensible decisions, also for instance noting kindness to others and/or responsibility shown for anything, however small. Some children find praise difficult (see Section XII).

- Positive reward programmes (discussed in Section XIV) provide regular opportunities for self-esteem enhancement in the secondary school.
- Increased positive eye-contact from the teacher to the child will also raise his self-esteem.
- The teacher repeats the child's words back to him to show him, he has been heard and understood.
- The teacher makes it clear it is understood when the child is making an effort even if he gets the 'answer' wrong.
- Letters home highlighting his good characteristics can affect how he is treated there.
- Time should be made for the child to talk to class teacher/tutor/year head so that attempts to make him feel known as an individual can be based on fact.

On the weekly sheets the success of this strategy will be indicated by a reduction in the frequency of 'flare-ups'. A reduction in intensity will follow. Maintain the programme for six weeks to effect change.

3. Tight schedule at home

Is there a tight schedule at home, where adults' work regimes dominate? This may include a very early morning start, too much time alone. The late return of adults means the child's opportunities for company and support from his parents are reduced. Carers may be pushing themselves too hard on punishing regimes of long working hours, having little energy left to respond to the child's needs at weekends and other free times.

Child's needs
The child needs understanding and recognition of the difficulties he deals with. He also needs his regime to adjust so that it is more comfortable even if it cannot be ideal.

Strategy
It is possible that the carers do not realise the connection and may be able to adjust aspects of the child's week if school is able to gently explore this with them. They may not be able or willing to change.

- Keep the weekly sheets.
- Decide a number of 'goods' the child can *easily* attain.
- A programme can be created using a free creative activity with a valued friend as the reward.
- It is important to remember to give positive feedback to the carers if they make good changes that help their child in school.
- Teachers also need positive feedback if they adjust their style to help the child.
- Recurrence of difficult behaviour can mean that the good intentions of the adults have not been sustained.
- Increase the target gradually as success can be confidently expected.
- A praising letter home can be a powerful reward, especially if adults will agree to spend time with the child on receipt of the letter.

4. Replica of home situation

Sometimes unwittingly a teacher's style can be a replica of what the child finds difficult at home. For example:

- The very strict teacher – and a very strict home.
- The teacher who nags or shouts at times may make things especially difficult for children who are nagged and shouted at home too much.
- The very open-ended creative teacher who is consciously creating opportunities for decision-making may make the child under stress or with a muddled disorganised home life crave structure and direction.

It is important for the teacher to get honest feedback from a trusted colleague to the question 'am I part of the problem'? Sometimes in a secondary school one lesson will stand out as being difficult across the curriculum. This may be a faculty issue as this child is probably not the only one experiencing difficulties in that lesson.

Child's needs
He needs a balanced week that meets his needs with an understanding teacher while he is at school and recognition of the difficulties he is dealing with.

Teacher's needs
The teacher needs support to broaden the teaching style to be flexible to a wider range of needs.

Strategy
After discussion with a colleague, adjust style and monitor result on weekly sheets. A home visit may help in the information gathering for this type of change. See Section X.

5. Bullying

It is crucial that whole-school policies are adhered to in this area by everyone. Where a problem persists despite this:

Bullying – Most children who bully are being bullied by adults or children themselves or have been at some time. They are enacting learnt behaviour. Most 'bullies' have extremely low self-esteem.

Being bullied – The child may also be being bullied or overridden by adults or children in or out of school and has learnt to let this happen to him. However, bullying can also be targeted at children whose values are different from those of the bully or children who have aspects to their lives that the bully envies. This child may need a great deal of support to express his needs assertively.

Child's needs
He needs to learn skills to keep himself safe, without hurting others. He needs adults to intervene on his behalf and he needs to feel known as an individual and valued.

Strategy
- Are there Child Protection Issues? If so, follow the Child Protection Procedures.
- Arrange a meeting with parents where appropriate to facilitate change, taking care not to bring more trouble to the child's life.
- Support him with skills in building reciprocal friendships; see Section III.
- Explore 'bullying' issue in whole class, using the school approach or confidentiality, whichever suits the situation best, but show the child he was also able to change things for the better by expressing himself assertively.
- Put known bullies on intensive self-esteem enhancement programmes to help them change their behaviour and learn to express themselves skilfully. Nurturing bullies is a time-effective way to deal with bullying in a school. See Section VII, 2.

The child may have bottled up anger and resentment which he cannot express elsewhere. It is likely that his anger is justified but is coming out inappropriately, aimed at his peer group and/or teacher over small unrelated issues.

VIII Cannot 'bring himself to a state of calm'

Child's needs

He needs to learn to express his feelings so that he can be valued and not to 'take it out' on the wrong person.

It is often helpful to him for an adult to recognise that he actually is angry with someone else, probably with good reason, but not really with 'Darren who nicked his pen'. Being understood helps the child to accept a strategy from an adult.

He is probably uncomfortable when he cannot control himself and will welcome genuine help. He needs to be able to restore control over himself and feel proud of himself for doing it.

Strategies

The 'thinking chair'

> **Keypoint** – This is explained carefully to him when he is not upset.

The chair is introduced to the rest of the class or group in a way which ensures he does not 'lose face'. 'Michael is helping me with an experiment' or 'Michael is being very sensible, he's got a lot on his mind and he wants to learn to calm himself down'. The child is praised for calming himself.

In the secondary context the child can learn to do this with the tutor or year head and practise it himself in his own chair in lessons. A separate chair could be used in lessons such as English and maths where more time is spent with that teacher.

A child chooses a place in the class to have a special chair. He can ask to sit in this chair to calm himself down, or the teacher could say 'Do you need your chair Michael?' He is praised for asking for it. A timing device, i.e. a clock, an oven-timer with bell or large egg-timer is set and the child takes deep breaths, relaxes or counts to himself. He is also praised for saying what the problem was when he is calm. Most secondary pupils can obviously use an ordinary watch, but large egg-timers can be very calming.

At a second stage the child learns to count silently on his fingers, eventually leaving behind the timing device, and sees the teacher's delight and pride in him at this development. This means he can calm down anywhere.

A third stage might be to just silently count without even using the chair.

It can be very effective to let him 'overhear' you telling another adult 'in confidence' how he's 'grown up', when he makes even tiny steps of progress. He should also be praised and carefully listened to when he chooses to explain a difficulty to the teacher at an appropriate time.

In the secondary context, the child should experience his tutor's praise for reporting having calmed himself down independently during the day.

Recording progress

Keep weekly sheets to monitor success, which will show in a reduction of the frequency first. After that, the intensity of the expression of emotion will begin to reduce.

Decide carefully whether you want the child to know how he's getting on, or if you feel it is working well as it is and it may be that introducing him to the monitoring records might add an unnecessary complication.

> **Keypoint** – The aim is for him to have learnt new and successful emotional expression that he can generalise to all situations. Particularly, he should be able to calm down and explain the problem.

Tangible records and rewards

When should these be used? When you want the child to hear about the programme and to demonstrate his progress and success. You are helping the child collect evidence of his good times and to monitor himself. This can be linked to receiving the reward of a praising letter home that he helps you to word. The letters trigger opportunities for parents to respond positively to that child and to reduce the possibility of the child being targeted as a scapegoat for adult tensions. These work best when the child helps in the design.

It is important to be careful how the tangible record is eventually dispensed with. It must not appear that good behaviour brings less attention. Usually the child can say when he is ready to manage without it. This may be a long time after the teacher feels it is necessary.

For secondary pupils, see also Sections XIV and XV.

Some different styles of rewards
1. A 'John had a good day' letter. This could be for an agreed number of good sessions. Let him help you word it.
2. A 'John beat his target of "goods" today' letter.
3. A drawing by the child with spaces to be coloured in representing good sessions, with 'Well done John' written on it and signed by the class teacher. These should be photocopied for regular use until the end of term and dated by teacher on completion. This can be recorded on weekly sheets.

Secondary schools
See also the case study of an individual pupil's positive reward programme (Section XIV) in which this method is described.

Use an ordinary secondary school report card that pupils take to each lesson. Subject teachers either sign box (to avoid fraud) or write a 'good' comment if deserved. This is explained to the pupil when he is not upset.

(a) Year head or tutor set teacher colours 'good' squares with red felt-tip pen at appropriate and agreed intervals during the week.
(b) After the first week they count the 'goods' with the pupil and invite him to set a target number of 'goods' for the following week. The targets should be easily attainable.
(c) Praise letter goes home if target is achieved each week.
(d) Target must increase each week, or hold steady if agreed.
(e) Photocopies of weekly sheets act as records of progress, evidence of school action strategies, and a tangible sign for pupils. You may need to photocopy daily for the pupil who keeps losing it. He will get better organised.
(f) Subject teachers across the curriculum become aware of progress with colleagues.

Figures 3.1, 3.2, 3.3 and 3.4 provide examples.

Figure 3.1

Figure 3.1 was prepared with the child using a favourite toy for the picture. The trucks were coloured in for each good session. It is better to use a number rather than a daily record as this means there is no tension concerning not completing one each day. He takes one home every time five are coloured in. Eventually this could be achieved each day.

Figure 3.2 was drawn by a mainstream teacher for a five-year-old girl who had very difficult behaviour which was being affected by adjustments to her medication for severe epilepsy. She coloured in different sections and took them home each day. Her parents agreed to praise her for the coloured sections and ignore the blank ones.

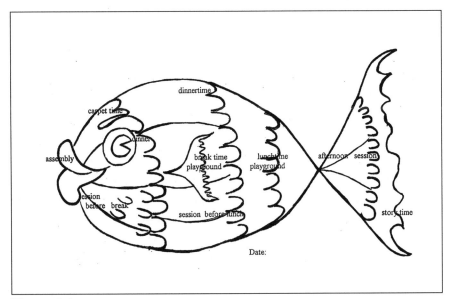

Figure 3.2

Date _____   Date _____

Dear Mr & Mrs Smith   Dear Mr & Mrs Jones

John has worked hard this week and has achieved his target of good sessions. We are very pleased and feel you can be proud of his effort.   John has had a good day. We are very pleased with him.

Yours sincerely   Yours sincerely

Mr Noble
Class teacher   Mr Noble
Class teacher

Figure 3.3   Examples of two letters older children have helped to word

Figure 3.4 shows what a child of ten drew for himself. Enough copies were photocopied for him to get one every day to the end of term. The rings were coloured in for good sessions. The sheets went home when full. Interestingly, his family were extremely busy, energetic people. Both parents worked very long shifts and the home ran with a high degree of organisation. It was a regime with little room for needs to be met outside the existing timetable. During the home visit it was clear that everything, including pets, garden, decoration, even 'bike cleaning' had allotted time. The family was eventually able to relax and this programme helped them to remember to praise him.

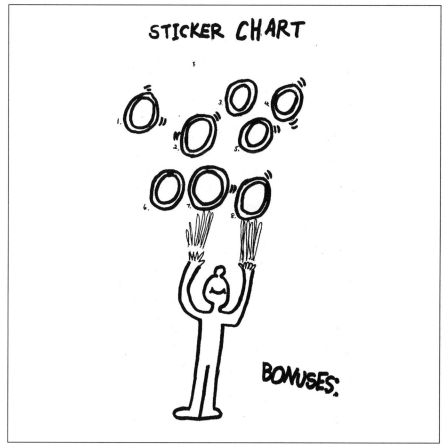

Figure 3.4   Sticker chart

This often indicates an anxious child who needs reassurance, or one who is 'distracted' for a variety of reasons. Sometimes children have their natural concentration interrupted constantly by siblings and adults, so that they have never experienced the joy of extended concentration.

IX Resists absorption in on-task work or cannot work without one-to-one support from an adult

Child's needs

He needs to learn to enjoy problem solving and concentrating peacefully without feeling anxious. He needs to feel praised and appreciated for learning this new way of behaving.

Strategy

1. The teacher prepares work, possibly with SENCO support, that the child can definitely complete without adult intervention. In the secondary context this is most practical in English or maths where more lessons per week take place. This may mean preparing the work at a consolidation level of difficulty for the start of this intervention.
2. Observation has determined how long the child would normally concentrate already: this might be as little as one minute.
3. The teacher engages the child in the following project without loss of face. 'John is helping me with an experiment' or 'John wants some help to improve his work'.
4. The child understands that the project is to help him and include him not to shame him or 'police' him.
5. He feels his increased 'absorption' is due to his own efforts.
6. There may be a group of children in the class who would benefit from joining in.

To proceed

1. Agree with the child a length of time you know he can be successful.
2. Choose a way, together, of recording it. For example, egg timer, oven timer with buzzer, child's own watch alarm or classroom clock.
3. Prepare a folder of consolidating work that the teacher knows the child can complete without adult intervention. For example:

- work sheets at current success level
- multiple choice
- completion of sentences
- comprehension – questions with sentences started
- last reading-book pages photocopied with gaps blanked out to fill in
- number worksheets at success level.

For younger children joining dot pictures or colouring would also be appropriate.

It is important that *no* coaching is required in this work. There should be no reason to call the teacher or ask any other child a question. At other times in the day the child does his normal work with the help he requires.

4. The child might choose to start off sitting alone to do this.
5. The child works for the agreed period of time. The teacher moves round the room attending to other children. The child puts his hand up when the buzzer goes or the sand runs through.
6. The teacher comes back to the child, praises him, makes good eye contact, and says 'well-done' to the group or individual involved. The teacher comments positively on the amount done and the quality of the work.
7. Teacher says 'Good, ready to try again? Off you go'. Teacher attends to others again but always returns when the buzzer sounds.
8. When success is established at this unit of time the teacher introduces the idea of progress to an agreed longer time – the two minute egg timer or another five minutes on the oven timer.
9. Gradually increase the time, within success level, until the child can remain absorbed for an appropriate length of time for his age and ability.
10. It may now be appropriate to introduce very gradually work that requires the child to think for himself more. Praise should be given for all independent decisions made by the child even if he made a 'wrong' decision. 'Well done for thinking that through by yourself John, but actually the right answer is ...'
11. When you feel the child is ready to take advantage of the offer, say 'You're doing really well now, we don't need the timer, just put your hand up if you need help'. Be careful to keep coming back anyway at the level of his last unit of timed success.

Record the success of this strategy on the weekly sheets as described in Step 1.

X Deterioration in child after time at home

You may need more information before you can proceed. If the deterioration is intense are there Child Protection Issues? If so, follow Child Protection Procedures. If not so intense, consider whether parents would find it helpful to talk through management difficulties with the school.

Child's needs

There is no simple formula for what a child needs from their home. However, to feel known and valued by the group we grow up in is a deep human need. Many different family styles provide this care successfully. Sometimes children's changing needs are not responded to effectively.

Strategy

Home visit
Much can be gained by the tutor set teacher involved visiting the child's home, so that the parents are more relaxed and the context of the child's life becomes clearer. The tutor set teacher may wish to arrange this visit jointly with the SENCO or year head. It should be a relaxed, friendly meeting. An appointment should be made a reasonable amount of time in advance, with the option of refusing if the carer would rather see you at school.

Aims of a home visit
  (a) To establish an understanding, accepting relationship with parents.
  (b) To include them in the team of adults who are going to help their child.
  (c) To explore discrepancies and stresses in the child's life.
  (d) To gather information that will help build an accurate profile of the child's life, so that an appropriate programme of rewards can be formulated.

Aspects that a home visit will help to clarify
It may be helpful to look at this after a visit. It is *not* a questionnaire to be used during a visit!

  1. Are basic physical needs regularly provided for:

  • food?
  • peaceful place to sleep?
  • normal supply of appropriate clothing?
  • access to adequate washing facilities?

  2. Is the home atmosphere a positive or a negative force in the child's life? Is it:

  • chaotic?
  • tense?
  • closed (inaccessible to outsiders)?
  • open, in a friendly way?
  • too open?
  • violent?
  • organised?
  • calm?
  • loving?
  • cold?
  • angry?

3. What are the family relationships like?

   - How do people speak to each other?
   - Do the parents let the child speak?
   - Is there uncomfortable rivalry between any family members?
   - Do people 'put the child down' a lot?
   - How does the family solve problems?
   - Do they smile and feel relaxed?
   - If one parent lives separately are they supportive and in regular contact? How often?
   - What role do the grandparents play?
   - Does the family enjoy his naughtiness?
   - Is there a big difference in attitude towards the child from each parent?
   - Does the child play an adult role with either of his parents or both, i.e. protective/parental/overseeing/equal partner?
   - What are their expectations of the child when he is an adult, and are these realistic?

4. What is the regime of the child's week like?

   - Does he spend a lot of time doing paid/unpaid work?
   - Does this affect his resting times?
   - Does he play and relax with his peers?
   - Does the child spend a lot of time with adults?
   - Does the child spend a lot of time alone?
   - Does he attend clubs, do sporting activities or hobbies regularly?
   - Is he supported in planning his week?

5. How is it that unwanted behaviour continues?

   - Is he being difficult to manage at home?
   - Are clear limits defined for the child?
   - Does someone else in the family benefit in some way from the bad behaviour?
   - Are there simple changes that could have been made to improve the situation that are not made? Why not?
   - What are the consequences of a broken family rule?
   - Do the children know the 'family rules'?
   - Are consequences and sanctions age appropriate and broadly similar to other homes?
   - Are all children in the family given equally positive attention?
   - How is the child praised and rewarded for good behaviour? What form does this take?

6. What else do you feel is important in this home?

7. Do you understand more about the pattern you observed on the weekly sheets?

- Do the child's needs seem clearer to you?
- Does the pattern fit into one of the categories described in this document?
- Do you have a clearer picture of how you can help him?

XI Works well on structured work sheet but not on open-ended creative work

This is common in distressed children. They probably feel rather like an adult would feel if they'd had a divorce, five house moves, a bereavement and were then asked to learn Russian at night school! If the work is structured, and gives success, that adult might be able to move slowly forward, but asked to write a creative piece might feel 'I can't'. Difficulty in this area can also be the result of very low self-esteem and confidence in decision-making. See also Section VII No. 2.

Child's needs

He needs to feel secure and to work towards developing the good decision-making skills required for creative work.

Strategy

Gentleness is appropriate, so structure creative activities for the child into simple steps. Be pleased with the results and highlight with praise any endeavour to be original. It may even be that the use of seemingly 'boring' work sheets that provide a high success level for the child will be appropriate to re-engage him in creative activities.

Creative writing
Give a list of questions to answer to lead his ideas forward in smaller steps than you might normally do for a child of his age and ability.

Art
Draw some examples and if necessary let him copy one. Draw an outline for him and let him complete it. Praise everything he adds.

Open-ended problems (maths, science, etc.)
Don't leave him anxiously seeking solutions. The educational benefit of discovering for himself during distressed periods of life does not necessarily outweigh the benefit of security in the learning situation and the comfort of success.

It may be that praise embarrasses the child. The language of praise may be unfamiliar to him. This usually accompanies very low self-esteem. It may be that the child cannot believe praise directed at him and mistrusts the motive of those delivering it. He may fear being exposed as the butt of a joke. Ordinary praise for one child may sound gushing and exaggerated to another.

XII Child appears to find praise difficult to accept

Child's needs

The child needs to learn that positive feedback about him can be true and trusted.

Strategy

- Begin with emotionally cool statements which confirm positive actions by the child. The more vulnerable the child the 'cooler' the praise should be. 'Not bad' delivered with respect can be a first acceptable step towards helping the child feel comfortable with praise.
- Pick tangible examples of the child's improved or good performance to direct the cool praise at. For example, a piece of work may not be as good as others in the class, but it is obviously better than his early work. Show the child both pieces while you deliver the respectful praising remark.
- Evidence praise of his actions: 'I saw you helping the new boy find the playground – when others left him behind – I was pleased.'
- Highlight and evidence characteristics you want him to develop more: 'That looks good, checking your homework book before you go home.'

Measure progress in this area by moving the remarks to a broad average script gradually.

If you have identified a pattern not mentioned above and have designed a strategy to help the child learn new skills – run it for at least three to six weeks, keeping weekly record sheets to record the effect of the strategy.

XIII Other patterns than those mentioned

> **Keypoint** – If the problem is reducing, i.e. if there are more good sessions or less intense behaviour, continue with the strategy.

Count 'outbursts' as improved if they happen less often. If they are not reducing after six weeks adjust the programme. If you are still not sure how to proceed, consider the following:

(a) Do you need more information? Try filling out the chart on Figures 3.5 and 3.6 – Examine the interaction between the various aspects of the child's life.

(b) Do you need to make a home visit?

(c) Have you checked the child's medical condition/hearing/sight?

(d) Is the problem less intense than you thought?

(e) Has the intense behaviour failed to show up during the weeks of observation? Has anything changed in the child's life? If not, observe longer, keeping the sheets and noting changes in the child's life if the intense behaviour returns.

(f) Make any changes to your classroom organisation that may have occurred to you while doing this observation. Observe the effect of this on the problem.

(g) Consult the chart in Figure 6.1 (p. 67).

(h) Define in detail the problem as you then see it and present it with your detailed observations at the next planning meeting with your educational psychologist.

Decide whether the planned strategy needs 'classroom differentiation', or 'liaison with SENCO' in the same way as you would for a learning difficulty. If you feel it is now appropriate to 'involve outside agencies as appropriate', ask parents to sign the appropriate forms, and if necessary discuss with the educational psychologist at your next planning meeting.

When you have designed the strategy, record it for the Code of Practice and run it for six weeks.

XIV Strategy for improving the behaviour of the six to eight most difficult pupils across a year group in a secondary school

This project should last at least one term. Pupils meet in a weekly group with the year head and one other teacher. This works well if tutor set teachers are involved in learning about the successes of the project and/or being the other teacher in the group. This also has career development potential. This project can be adapted for primary schools.

The pupils are all put on positive reward programmes. Parents are involved by having the strategy explained to them at the start and by receiving letters noting their child's success on the way through.

1. Select the six to eight pupils that use up most of your time with behavioural issues.
2. Inform the parents.
3. Put the pupils all on positive reward programmes.
4. Establish a weekly meeting with them and one other teacher.

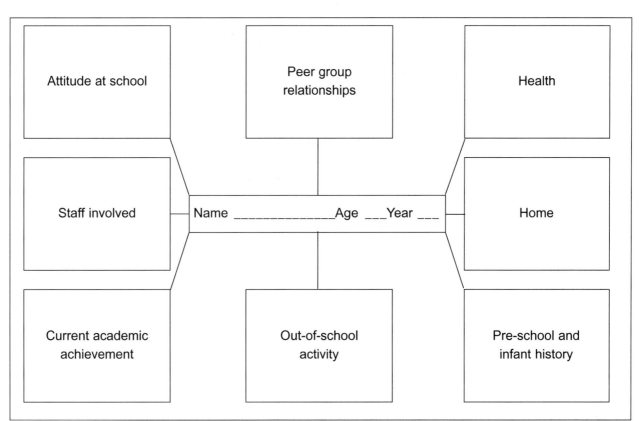

Figure 3.5   Chart for filling in what is known about a child

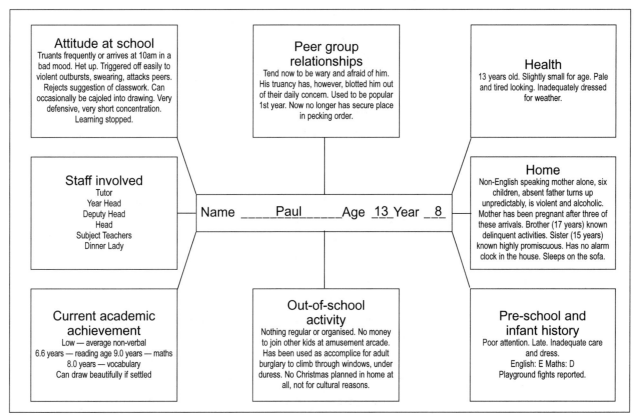

Figure 3.6   A 13-year-old boy at mainstream secondary school

5. Prepare enough 'well done' letters to cover each pupil, every week until the end of term.
6. Normal school rules apply throughout.
7. Dealing with unfair situations.
8. Miracles *can* happen!

See the following paragraphs for detailed descriptions of each of the points outlined above.

Strategy for behaviourally difficult pupils across a year group in a secondary school

1. Selecting the pupils
Select the pupils who take up most of your time. They can be a mixed group of boys and girls of withdrawn behaviour and/or disruptive pupils, and pupils with attendance problems. It is not recommended to use this strategy with more than eight in a group that meets to share success.

2. Informing the parents
Invite the parents in to explain to them:
   (a) This project is to help their child to control himself.
   (b) Letters will be sent home praising the pupil when their targets are achieved and parents should try and show the child they are pleased about these.
   (c) Normal school rules will apply throughout the project. This could mean a child achieves his target and gets his letter home in a week when some other misdemeanour has meant a detention or other sanction. The project is monitoring long-term improvement and is not invalidated by episodes of negative behaviour.

3. Putting them each on positive reward programmes
All pupils are given standard school weekly report sheets for subject teachers to comment on their lesson performance throughout the week. These report sheets are used as follows:

   (a) Each day the pupils show the year head, or tutor set teacher, their report sheet.
   (b) The year head or tutor colours in any squares marked 'good' in red felt-pen and gives praise and encouragement to gain more of these and asks the pupil to elaborate on how they got 'goods' in different lessons.

Negative remarks are to be left uncoloured and unreferred to. If the child shows interest in discussing negative sessions, the year head blocks the conversation by saying 'We're not here to discuss that: I want to know how you managed to get the "Goods".'

An appropriate target of 'goods' is set and increased by one every week it is attained.

Attainment of the weekly target is rewarded with a letter home (see Figure 3.7).

Setting the target

This is done in consultation with the pupil. He should be encouraged to go through his timetable and count only the lessons he knows he can definitely get a 'good' in. There is always at least one lesson, usually several. The targets should be individually selected with each pupil. It is made clear that the 'game' is that it goes up one every week.

If any week the target is not achieved, it stays the same as the last successful one for another week. Do not increase at more than one a week even if he earns far more 'goods' than the targets.

(a) Subject teachers are simply asked to either write 'good' or fill the space with their initials.

(b) No special behaviours are targeted. The 'good' should represent each teacher's own concept of good.

(c) No threats should be made about getting a 'good' or not. If the pupil does not meet the 'good' standard of the teacher, he will just initial the form in that space.

(d) Subject teachers are informed that normal school sanctions apply throughout the programme and no special treatment is required for this pupil.

See the case study of an individual behaviour programme at the end of this section.

Parents' name   **Date**

Parents' address

Dear ....

**Once again I am really happy to let you know how
pleased I am with .... this week. Yet
again she has made a great effort and achieved her target of good
lessons.**

Yours sincerely

Head of Year

Figure 3.7   Example of a letter home

4. Establishing a weekly meeting

These seem most effective with two teachers. Previous groups of pupils of both sexes have felt that a male and female adult works best if it can be arranged. It is also helpful for them to witness two teachers listening to them, helping them and praising them for progress. Decide if you want a 'closed' group with no new members joining or an 'open' group which would have changing members.

Pupils are encouraged to discuss how the project is going and how they are getting over any problems they have met.

It is often the case that such pupils have difficulties outside school also and they may find it helpful to have peer support from this group in how they deal with these. Sometimes a pupil will not be sure if he can comply with the whole thing and the peer group support can make the difference. A discussion about confidentiality helps people feel safe to talk.

Often in these groups I have heard pupils say they find school less tiring when they are 'good'! They also tend to be more relaxed and so start to make friends more successfully.

You also get an opportunity to monitor how their carers are reacting to receiving the letters home. This means that school can compensate with more positive attention if parents appear to have forgotten to do that.

Here is an extract from a secondary school Year 8 Pupil Support Group:

> Their conversation then moved off so that it was between them more and they were soon discussing the level of caring from each of their parents. Most of them felt their mothers cared more and it soon became clear that only one of them still lived with his natural father. They each seemed quite surprised that this common factor existed.
>
> Robert was immediately able to describe his idea of a good Dad – 'One who is interested in his family, who takes them to the beach for the day, who does things with you'. They all agreed with this image, adding that he should stand up for his children and not be violent. Philip then explained that his natural father visited at unpredictable times and this caused trouble in the family. His stepfather adamantly didn't want Philip 'picked up and let down' like this and was very strongly against the visits. Philip however had mixed feelings about the visits and could remember a time when he and his natural father went canoeing together and had good times doing this.
>
> He did not think he could ask his stepfather to go canoeing with him when one of the boys suggested this. Steven advised him to make friends with the Dad he had living with him. Steven added that he did not know who his natural father was and that this sometimes bothered him. He also described a violent row between his stepfather and his mother during which he had run to his grandmother's house and phoned the police. When asked if things were better now he replied 'Oh yes, he knows now that I won't put up with that, he respects me now

and treats me like an adult'. This feeling of being a protector over their mothers and an overseer of any new partners was a common source of pressure for them. Justin mostly listened this week, he seemed depressed and almost afraid to speak. Shane made many attempts to disrupt the session and seemed determined to keep the conversation superficial; when it was suggested to him that this was his way of avoiding painful issues he agreed with a very honest smile and sat with his head in his hands until the end of the session. They talked about being afraid to cry and that when they got angry other issues got muddled in with it. This meant they may have a fight with another pupil about something small but the level of anger was much more than the situation warranted and their anger about personal issues got involved. The main issues in this session seem to be the link between violence and anger and their roles as parenting children.

5. Letters home

It is important that these letters are treated with proper status. A pupil once noticed that 'good' letters had 2nd class stamps but letters of complaint were sent by 1st class mail!

These are particularly effective if the pupils help you to word them. Their choice of words often gives you clues to the pupils' difficulties. It may be that different pupils need differently worded letters or they may all be happy with one. This is not onerous to arrange and can make a huge difference to the success of the project.

I would suggest making enough copies to cover every pupil on a programme for every week to the end of the term. This means that you never run out or feel you cannot find the time to comply with your part of the bargain on a Friday afternoon when the sheet is complete.

The project is most likely to fail if you let them down and do not send a letter they have earned. The Elton Report ('Discipline in Schools') found such letters to be a powerful reward. They are learning to trust you and have completed their part of the bargain. It may be hard to win their trust if you disregard this.

6. Normal school sanctions apply throughout

No special arrangements are made. If school rules are broken normal sanctions apply. This means a pupil could have a fight on Monday and be suspended for a day and still meet his target of 'goods' by the end of the week, and he has earned his letter home, noting that he has achieved his target. This is fine and not as contradictory as it seems, as long as everyone understands the project. The behaviour programme is a long-term intervention to improve school behaviour, and it makes no claims to eliminate difficulties overnight. The child may have taken 14 years to be like he is and is not going to change immediately.

However, he has agreed to set a target with you that he believes he can achieve and you have agreed to reward that with a letter to his parents, noting the event. Everyone must stick to this agreement. The teacher running the project may be the same person who has to discipline the pupil for the misdemeanour. A clear distinction is made between the two things and it is emphasised that the incident does not jeopardise the eventual success of the programme.

Disinterest in the misdemeanour will help as will a matter-of-fact style of dealing with administering the sanction. It is worth making clear at these times that such sanctions are the pupil's responsibility and in his control to avoid. It can be helpful to remind him of times on the programme when he has controlled himself and been mindful of consequences. Try to avoid the school's response to a misdemeanour being of a higher status, more public, more excitable and more intense than its response to his efforts to improve.

It may be helpful to remind parents of the above by writing on the letter something like 'a difficult week but steps towards the long-term goals of this project are still being made successfully'.

7. Dealing with unfair situations

A year head or tutor set teacher will know there are some lessons where it will be almost impossible for the pupil to get 'good' written on the sheet by a particular teacher. A variety of reasons will create these situations but they may be outside the brief of the year head or tutor set teacher to change.

One such class from my experience was that of a very disorganised French teacher who screamed at the children and rarely got any group working at all. It was a supply teacher who would finish at the end of the following term.

The behaviour programme is the one featured in the case study at the end of this section. We put it to the pupil that life often throws up difficult situations that have to be solved. To reach his new target he had to get a 'good' in French. It was one of the last subjects not to be coloured in red each week. We laughed with him about various ploys he might try, while being careful in our remarks about the difficulties. I happened to meet him in the corridor after that lesson and he shouted delightedly, punching the air in triumph, 'Hey Miss, I got a "good" in French!' Amazed, I asked him how he did it; he replied 'I kept me gob shut!'

8. Miracles can happen too!

Sometimes a particular subject that is the last to go 'red' will suddenly become a 'good' lesson. It may have less to do with something specific the child has done and more to do with that particular teacher realising that they are the only one not getting a 'good' from this child. Perhaps they organise differently or see different qualities in the child – it is a mystery, but one with a good outcome!

Case study – individual pupil's positive reward programme

Organisation

This was a Year 8 pupil. The early organisation was begun by a year head who was later taken ill. The pupil for this project was identified by her. Her role was however most effectively filled by his tutor set teacher. This project was intended to show use of a standard weekly report sheet used as a positive reward programme and taking no more teacher time than in its usual use.

The pupil

Robert was thirteen and a half when he joined the school in the second term of Year 8. He had arrived in a highly distressed state. Family traumas, which had been considerable, resulting in divorce, had severely unsettled him. He had lived first with his mother then his father, then went back to his mother as concern grew about the level of care and support he was receiving. He had witnessed many violent scenes and had been drawn into these frequently. The last of these had resulted in Robert being stabbed as he tried to defend his mother. His first address in the county was a family refuge. His school behaviour took the form of being extremely disruptive in lessons; he was prone to sudden aggressive attacks on other children, highly attention-needing and seemingly at times uncontrollable. In contrast to this, he would respond as an unhappy but warm-hearted boy in a one-to-one situation, and would discuss with little encouragement a series of frightening and distressing events from his family life.

It was noted in the initial observation of Robert that he showed concern about improving his relationship with his mother. 'She has a go at me every day and I m fed up with it.' He had said this during one conversation in which he appeared worn down with worry. It was decided to support this boy with a positive reward scheme that would highlight his good behaviour and reward it with a letter home to his mother to inform her when he made progress through an effort to control himself.

School was also being informed at this time that Robert was getting into trouble outside school in various and very worrying ways. He put a hose through a door on his paper round and turned on the tap. Glue-sniffing, alcohol and a robbery with a violent attack were included, as well as stealing from friends and being found trespassing on British Rail land, dangerously walking along the track. He was arrested in Week 8 (see Figure 3.8). Social Services already had contact with the family and during the following half term he was referred for support from the Department of Family and Child Psychiatry.

Aims behind the intervention

1. To demonstrate the use of a standard weekly report sheet as a positive reward programme.

2. To encourage a very disturbed pupil, in trouble outside school and in, to keep lesson times and break times 'safe' in terms of his behaviour and by working to his potential.
3. To preserve a learning environment for the other pupils.

Structure of the intervention

Each week in the tutor set period he was given a fresh standard report sheet. This had previously been commented on in the usual way and sometimes this meant that particularly bad lessons were discussed and disapproved of. In the new programme, the previous week's total number of 'good' lessons was discussed with him, the 'goods' would be counted, and a new target for 'goods' set. If he had reached the target of the previous week it was increased to beat that figure and he was given a short letter to take home to his mother. This letter praised him for making an effort, stated that he had reached his target and that school were pleased with him for doing so. He helped word the letter and added 'You should be proud of him'!

Each day at the end of school he brought his report sheet to his tutor teacher, who would praise him for the 'goods' he had received, colour them in red felt-tip pen and put the day's total of 'goods' in the last column. Particular interest would be shown in exactly how he had managed to get these 'goods', and he would be encouraged to try these techniques in other lessons that he found difficult. He would be encouraged to think about why he found some lessons easier and what different elements existed. Particular enthusiasm would be shown from the teacher if he managed to achieve a 'good' for one of these more difficult lessons.

The teacher's attitude to 'bad comments' would be to show a total lack of interest; no attention was given as to the details of how a 'bad comment' was obtained or in the detentions or lines that had been received. If he showed interest in getting attention for these and wanted to talk about what had happened in a bad lesson, the teacher would reply, 'That's not what we're here to talk about, Robert, I'm really more interested to know how you got the "good" for such and such. That was a difficult lesson for you, tell me all about it, how did you do it?' In this way he should become aware that the adult attention he desperately needs is available, but only for increasing his good behaviour.

Evaluation

The tutor set teacher was most enthusiastic about this technique and gave the following answer when asked if he would feel 'able and/or inclined to operate this type of programme with another pupil': 'This was the first time I have done anything like this and the effects were so dramatic that it would be something I would resort to once I had identified a pupil as being someone for whom normal sanctions would not work ... I would certainly wish to repeat this'. The teacher's use of the word 'dramatic' refers to his day-to-day contact with the boy as he found him far more accessible than previously.

Robert's scores had been erratic between the end of April and the beginning of May. It is quite common to see an initial improvement followed

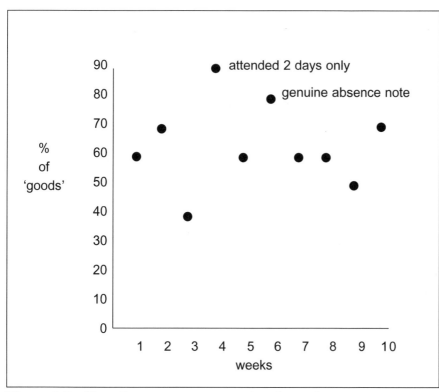

Figure 3.8   How the programme went each week

by a sharp drop in score, indicating a return to the old behaviours when it becomes difficult to achieve the reward. It is often the case that people give up behaviour projects at this stage claiming that behaviour modification did not work or even made the child worse. However, after the drop the score should then rise gradually and the improvement should be maintained. In this case the programme begins as normal but the sudden drops in Weeks 5 and 9 are more uneven than usual in a programme where no other dramatic changes have taken place in the subject's life. It is therefore reasonable to look for other elements that might be influencing the score in order to adapt the procedure to suit the individual situation and to steady the scores. I asked the teacher why he thought this was. I had interpreted these uneven scores as being the result of Robert's getting arrested for the robbery during that time; however the teacher felt he could identify a period of two or three weeks during which his own workload was higher than usual as well as a couple of days of lost report sheets. He commented, however, that Robert's overall average of above 65 per cent 'goods' in all but two weeks, was an outstanding achievement for this boy. The teacher had been away on a course and this had meant a couple of weeks recently without the programme. Robert apparently 'plummeted especially in certain key lessons'. His life outside school was still very unstable and he appeared not yet ready to manage without being monitored.

Another spin-off from this programme was that the tutor set teacher had developed a highly supportive tutor relationship with this boy. This can be seen in the following extract from the questionnaire. 'Robert was in line for a place in the sports day team for athletics ... my colleague unfortunately decided that the form should vote on this ... although I haven't heard what the result was I'm pretty sure it will be very one-sided, once again another "slap in the face" from one more quarter.'

Robert also attended the counselling group for second years and said in it, 'I want to control myself but I think I need some help in how to do it'. He also said he would attend a group after school to carry on the work he felt he had started. Robert also developed a friendship in the group with a boy who had previously been school refusing. They supported each other to long-term success.

Report sheets used in this way do appear to support pupils like Robert. It is a good technique for building a relationship between a tutor and a difficult pupil. Each member of the counselling group could probably have benefited from monitoring their efforts to 'control themselves' during the week. Using these two strategies together provides a strong positive message of support leading to improvement for those pupils in a year who cannot 'control themselves' without extra help. It is also no more time-consuming than other methods that year heads might use.

XV Strategy for improving the behaviour of a class that has become difficult to teach

This project can be adapted for primary classes.

1. The case study presented in this section was coordinated by a tutor set teacher throughout.
2. An initial introduction to the scheme was carried out in a tutor set period.
3. A letter was sent to parents describing the structure and purpose of the scheme.
4. The pupils voted to retain the scheme after a period of time as they had come to enjoy the resulting workplace atmosphere.
5. The tutor set teacher was delighted with his improved relationship with them.

Case study of a second year tutor set positive reward programme

Organisation

This piece of work was set up with a Year 8 tutor set teacher who was concerned about the classroom behaviour of his tutor set. He had received many reports from subject teachers that his tutor set were noisy, rude and extremely difficult to settle and to teach. He had already asked teachers to name trouble-makers in the day book and had also sent a standard class report sheet round with them. This will be discussed later in the evaluation of this programme. The tutor set teacher approached the outreach team from a special school for behaviourally difficult pupils and suggested that they were included in the classes seen by them in the initial phase of observation.

The class was observed for one full day by the Special School teacher who then met the teachers who taught them. Their ability and attainment levels were considered and an attempt was made to look at the central figures in the classroom difficulties.

It was decided to devise a positive reward scheme for the whole class which was simple for subject teachers to administer. The plan was to try a scheme, monitor the effect and then to decide, with involvement from the pupils, whether to continue or to adapt the programme.

The class

This tutor set of 25 Year 8 pupils had been identified as the most troublesome Year 8 group. It is possible, due to the wide ability range among them, that, to a school new to teaching mixed ability, they represented the most worrying aspect of the change, until the teachers developed individual work programmes and group work studies.

In the period of change this lively and demanding group, with its wide range of need, stretched the resources of the teachers they met and showed little patience or willingness to provide a peaceful learning atmosphere for each other.

The class was observed for a day as they went from class to class, so that the dynamics in the group could be seen building up between lessons on their own and with teachers.

Notes from the day's observations

This class has a wide range of ability with two pupils identified as having special learning needs and four or five pupils whose achievement and ability is at the very top end of the year. Three of the group were identified by the year head as within the seven candidates out of the whole year most in need of the support group discussed in the previous section. They had acquired a reputation for being a very difficult class to teach.

Interestingly, they were a very pleasant group of pupils to spend a day with. Unlike another Year 8 class observed who had a lot of in-fighting and cliques among them, they were good to each other during the day. This actually made them a more difficult group to penetrate for each classroom teacher as they went round. They were extremely lively, sparky and demanding but seemed unsure of their group identity. There was strong evidence in their conversation of parental interest, high expectations and an element of wanting to do well at school and afterwards.

The most difficult aspect of this effervescent group was in calming them into silence at the start of lessons long enough to give instructions. However, when presented with individually relevant material they eventually worked hard and enjoyed praise and evidence of progress. Sessions where the whole class were expected to move at the same pace generally went less well.

They have recently been 'de-streamed' and they seem unsettled and unsure of what this means in terms of the school's expectations of their ability level. If any teacher gives the group feedback as to the nature of the group there is a level of interest shown that is noticeably deep. One feels they want to know what it means to be in this group.

When the class is split up for activities such as craft, drama, etc., only one of the pupils was identified as being difficult, but together it must be said they were a force to be reckoned with and presented a challenge to even the most organised and experienced teachers.

Aims behind the intervention

1. To work with the tutor set teacher to pass on the theory and method of a positive reward programme with a full class.
2. To help a class of Year 8 pupils to develop autonomous decision-making skills in relation to their behaviour in class.
3. To create an ethos within this tutor set where appropriate learning could take place.

Structure of the intervention

This intervention was a positive reward programme designed to help individuals to receive feedback on good behaviour in class. The theory behind it was that of behaviour modification. The teacher from the Special School arranged to attend the tutor set period of the class each week to help the class teacher introduce the scheme and to advise where necessary.

A class list was prepared and opposite each name a grid was drawn, containing one square for each of the 28 lessons that the class had as a full group. It was explained to the class, by the tutor set teacher, that they would receive a tick for any lesson in which they were absolutely perfect in behaviour. This was discussed at length, with the class being asked what they felt that meant. They offered a wide range of excellent behaviours such as 'working as hard as you can', 'paying attention', 'being quiet when asked to be', 'working properly in groups', 'remembering books, etc'.

It was generally agreed that they knew what a committed, cooperative contribution to a lesson meant. It was mentioned that it was not merely being asleep in the back row and not annoying anyone! Having satisfied ourselves that they understood what they were to get a tick for, they were then told that the space would be filled with a cross if they did not get one.

At the end of the week, in the tutor set period, the ticks would be counted up and each person be encouraged to beat their own best. No rewards were discussed, although housepoints for beating their own best had been discussed between the Special School teacher and the tutor set teacher to be possibly introduced later. It was decided to run the scheme for a week to see how it went and to see the initial range of scores they would achieve. It was also felt from the observation day that the feedback itself both to the group as a whole and to individuals was responding to a strong need and as such was rewarding in itself.

The tutor set teacher explained the scheme to the subject teachers, making it clear to them that they must be 'ruthless' with the ticks and only award them for individuals who had achieved an extremely high standard of commitment to the lesson offered, i.e. making their individual best effort with the work; engaging with the tasks set; being sociable; being organised to the best of their individual ability and keeping classroom rules.

It was pointed out to the children that these rules might differ slightly from room to room but if they wanted to get a tick they had to be able to work out those differences and respond to them.

It could be said that it is unfair to make it so hard but the reality in school is that to achieve, children do need to solve these problems. The aim of the scheme was to help this class respond more positively to mainstream school. This means building learning relationships with a large group of adults who are all different.

It can be seen that there is also a challenge to the content of the lesson in a scheme of this nature. If a teacher is asked to identify children who have worked to the best of their individual ability, there is an assumption made that the work they are being given is individually relevant. It would soon be apparent to a teacher giving a class lesson that moved at the speed of the middle group only to a mixed-ability group, for instance, that giving a score on attitude to the pupils at the two extremes of ability becomes unfair. It is clear that they could not work to the best of their ability if they were either not being stretched or could not do the work.

The intervention was run for one week and they then had a week without it to compare class behaviour. Discussion with the tutor set resulted in its being continued until the end of that half term, a further three weeks. At the end of that time the class voted to continue using the scheme in the next half term and beyond.

The tutor set teacher was extremely enthusiastic about his role with this group and his organisation of the intervention made it possible. This involved using his free lessons to discuss the theory behind the intervention with the Special School teacher, explaining it to his class and their teachers, preparing the class lists and using the tutor set period to praise high scorers, encourage problem-solving in low scorers, as well as answering pupils' and teachers' questions.

How the tutor set periods were spent
Week I

The tutor set teacher introduced the scheme to the class, and at separate times to the class teachers. The main difficulty both groups found was the emphasis on positive behaviour. It had to be continually reinforced that the cross simply filled a space with no tick in it and was not a 'bad' mark. They found it difficult to grasp the concept that we wished to highlight for the pupils what they did that was pleasing and on the right course for high achievement in school. It was later suggested by a pupil that the space should be filled by a 'nought' as it gave less attention to not getting a tick. Apart from showing a remarkable understanding of the nature of the scheme he had also noticed that some children and teachers had become more concerned about why a cross 'was given'.

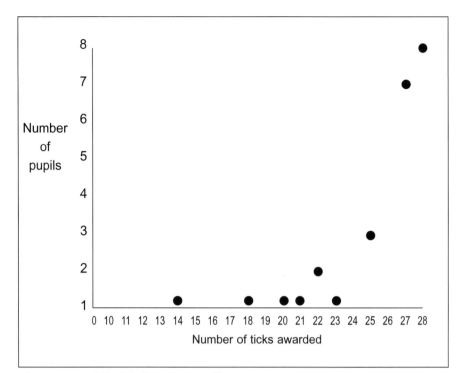

Figure 3.9 Week I (25–29 April)

This, in my own experience, is an extremely common stage in introducing a positive reward programme. Asking people to turn their thinking as it were 'inside out' is likely to take time, and one brief explanation is never likely to be enough. People need to be able to come back and say 'yes – but what if?...' Whenever I have heard people say, 'I tried behaviour modification and it didn't work,' I suspect that these questions have not been answered during the process.

The scheme was to operate for one week only starting from that tutor set time.

Week II

As this was a bank holiday there was no tutor set period this week and the scheme had not been intended to run for the second week. However, much comment was stimulated by the scheme with many more of the questions I mentioned before, coming from the parents now as well as the teachers and pupils! The parents of two girls had queried why their daughters had been 'given crosses'. It was explained again that they were only 'given' ticks – crosses simply filled the spaces if a tick was not awarded.

The average score, for the first week, of ticks out of the 28 lessons they spent together as a class, was 25. The scores were distributed as shown in Figure 3.9. Absences with a letter from parents were counted as ticks.

The pupils were very interested in each other's scores. It seemed a key issue to know who complied with school rules. This interest seemed in keeping with the original observation that this class was anxious to find its identity as a group. In fact 15 of the class scored very highly with seven of those only missing one tick.

The three boys who were suggested for the counselling group scored 18, 22 and another 22. They were not the lowest.

Week III

During the week without the scheme the old habits returned. The special school teacher talked to the class about what they found difficult, and how they felt they had scored the ticks they received. They were asked to discuss in four small groups whether they thought that the scheme helped them, what it was like without it and whether they should try it again. It also came out in this discussion that different teachers had different expectations of them and that behaviour that could get a tick in one room was not enough in another. They also discussed classes that groups of them found difficult.

This lively session was observed by their tutor set teacher. It was decided to use the scheme again for another week and, as the tutor set period was the first session of the class together, that the session we had just had should be scored even though they were not warned to be on their best behaviour. This meant that only eleven pupils gained a tick. We discussed with them how they had been 'caught out' and how in the end the plan was for them to control themselves with no scheme.

It was noted that class teachers had not awarded fewer than eighteen ticks and so the tutor set teacher saw each of them during that week to remind them to use it as a game played ruthlessly to the rules. They were further reminded that the score must represent accurately when the pupils were excellent and that not getting a tick did not incur punishment of any kind.

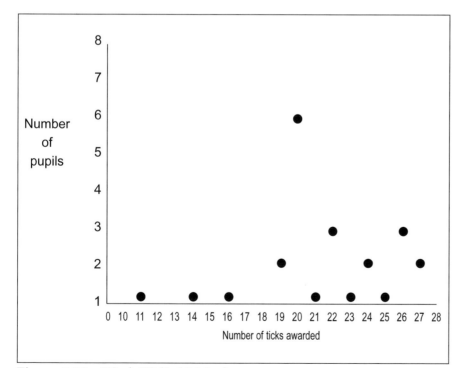

Figure 3.10   Week III (9–13 May)

Week IV

An effect of the tutor set teacher talking to the class teachers was noted in the scores for week III. They were much lower and the pupils said the teachers were making the ticks harder to get. This, of course, made it harder for them to beat their own best and it was decided that until everyone got used to using the scheme it would be difficult to compare the weeks' scores. However the pupils were interested in competing with each other and competing for a high score.

Figure 3.10 shows how fewer pupils have scored very high scores although pupils scoring 18 or less have only risen by one. In spite of the tougher regime five pupils managed to increase their score. The lowest number of ticks awarded in any one session was 15 which was still higher than the tutor set period by four ticks.

The pupils seemed really interested in the scheme at this time and were asking considered questions about various incidents through the week. One issue was that teachers were saying 'if you do that again you'll lose your tick' – as the children rightly pointed out no one has a tick until they've earned it by a perfect lesson. It was pleasing to see how well they had grasped its spirit. They also noted in the above example that if someone had done something which made their contribution less than excellent they had not earned a tick anyway. This sort of slip by staff is very common, I have found, when a scheme of this kind involves more than one or two teachers. It is unfortunately often the case that aspects of a scheme which 'threaten' to modify the attitude or behaviour of the teacher will be resisted by them in

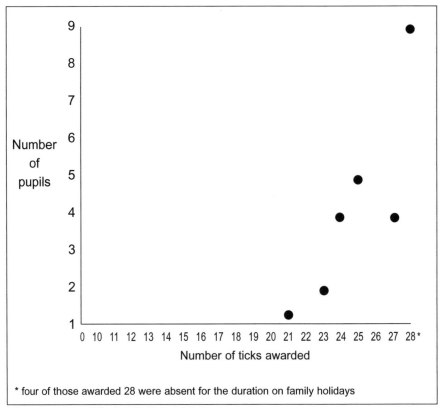

* four of those awarded 28 were absent for the duration on family holidays

Figure 3.11   Week IV (16–20 May)

spite of the obvious benefits for the class. This highlights the need to keep reminding staff of the theory behind an intervention of this kind and being available to answer their questions until the scheme is established.

I noted that, for the first time since my contact with them began, it was actually pleasant and interesting to spend a lesson with this class. They were always lively and funny but very hard work to keep on task. They now seem more relaxed and mature, and also seem to be beginning to appreciate the potential this scheme has for them.

Week V

There seems a genuine sign of progress during week IV with no one scoring less than 21 and all but one pupil beating his own last score. The lowest scorer has more than doubled his score. They are even more agreeable as a class than last week and voted to continue the scheme after the half term.

They were asked to write down what they would say to a friend who was about to begin a similar scheme. Here are extracts from their answers; only one boy gave a negative comment. Each pupil's three weekly scores are given in the brackets.

...'a good idea, I want to carry on and improve my scores (28, 21, 25) ... has helped a very lot people (28, 22, 27) ... it would be better if you had a mark for being average (27, 23, 28) ... I told my Mum I like school now (absent, 22, 26) ... it made people behave and work better (18, 19, 26) ... it is a good method of keeping order because people work hard for their ticks (27, 24, 25) ... had a big effect on the class, made everyone mostly behave but they let go sometimes (26, 22, 27) ... it makes you want to get a tick so you work well, it is a good thing to have (27, 22, 26) ... it is good because everyone is quiet because they want a tick (21, 22, 25)... it is alright because you know who the naughtiest is (20, 23, absent) ... it is good because it makes people better behaved (22, 19, 25) ... it is good because it makes us work a lot and be good (26, 25, 26) ... having the ticks is silly because it doesn't do anything at all (28, 22, 26) ... I think teachers should keep it to themselves if someone has lost their tick as they would play up for the rest of the lesson (27, 28, 28) ... a big difference, class works more and listens more (27, 28, 28) ... makes people work harder (27, 28, 28) ... the class is much quieter and gets more work done (28, 27, 27) ... it is a good idea because you are not bad in class (18, 14, 21) ... it made a lot of people's behaviour better (28, 26, 28) ... it makes the class behave and not be stupid to see what the teachers have to say at their behaviour (28, 27, 28) ... it is a good idea because it matters if they've been good or bad (26, 27, 24) ... it was a good idea people behaved better, it made the class quieter so we got on with our work better and everyone improved their score each week (28, 28, 28)'.

We have talked to this group, and given them group-focused discussion opportunities, about the benefits to each of them if the class as a learning group can provide an appropriate atmosphere for their lesson times. We have also presented them with an expectation that they will be ready to do this without support increasingly, so that by the start of Year 9 they will be able to work to their full potential for entry to their exam courses.

Evaluation

A questionnaire was sent to the tutor set teacher and to each of the subject teachers of the seven who taught them as a group. Four completed the questionnaire as requested and three of those felt the scheme had had a positive effect on the behaviour of the pupils as did the tutor set teacher. The remaining three returned the sheets filled in with one word answers, when clearly asked to elaborate. Interestingly, these had contradictory answers in spite of their brevity which suggested the classic defensive teacher response, 'this class are no trouble for me' when they are clearly a difficult group to educate appropriately. This highly defensive position demonstrates the points made about the de-skilling and threatening aspects of difficult pupils to a profession that has to develop its strategies for sharing problems.

The observation day could not support the suggestion that individually appropriate work was on offer more in these rooms than others; in fact the opposite was true. All these gave whole-class lessons in strong authoritative styles, which, while being effective as regards discipline, allowed little engagement from the group and did not recognise the group's wide ability range. Anyone who was trying to use group work, individual work or experimental learning styles found them to be very difficult to settle.

The class were, as a result of those strategies, 'no trouble for them', but it would seem that the aim should be to train the group so that more appropriate teaching methods can be used successfully.

One teacher flippantly replied 'pass' to Question 4, 'would you use this with another class?' having indicated earlier that the scheme had improved the behaviour of the class. One who answered 'I don't feel any real need for it', also answered the request for improvements to the scheme 'euthanasia for a few members of the class'.

Another who answered simply 'no' to Question 5 which asked about change in their relationship with the class, had already written 'They are more conscious of their behaviour' in answer to Question 1. When it is remembered what the pupils themselves have written about what the scheme means to them one can see the huge task involved in creating a climate for change. Any year head should be wary of being called in to encourage children to be contained by inappropriate lesson content. This is another area where teachers' support groups can be helpful. It must not be forgotten that it is stressful to give up defensive mechanisms.

This is not to say that the scheme should not be criticised and the questionnaire did invite criticism and provide room for it. Teachers were specifically asked to say why they would or would not use it with another class.

The other four teachers who filled in the questionnaire fully both praised and criticised but in a seemingly 'unthreatened' and helpful way.

I will now look at their answers. First of all to Question 1: 'In which ways would you say that the tick sheet for this tutor set has affected the class'.

One teacher felt that the workload had improved among pupils who previously took a long time to settle. Two of them felt that only some of the class cared about the scheme and others actively did not care. It is interesting that the teachers felt this and one actually said 'It was interesting that it really only affected the ones who generally would have got favourable comments before', when clearly the pupils' comments, and their voting unanimously to continue, contradicts this. The pupils may have 'acted' as if they didn't care.

Questions 2 and 3 asked if they could make any suggestions for improving the administration. One reply felt that one pupil only, with a stand-in for absences, should be responsible for it as it was often left in her room. One teacher suggested an extra sheet so that teachers could put general comments about the class as a whole. It had been noted of course that the class do need to establish a group identity, but in order to ensure that comments would give useful highlighting to the positive aspects of the group I feel much discussion would have to take place among the teachers. It was mentioned that this class had the usual class report sheet before this scheme and it had not changed the behaviour of the class. On the top of that sheet the tutor set teacher had written 'Any pupils who are noisy or disruptive, please list, any who are rude, please send to me'. He also left a space on the sheet for homework for the class to be filled in.

The old report sheets that were made available to me showed a very different class attitude to that which was being reported to the tutor set teacher. They received 26 out of 28 class 'goods'. This was most often simply the word 'good'. It certainly did not describe the class that I had spent a day with and did not make them a class that was easy to initially explain the scheme to as a visitor. It is also interesting that five teachers noted an improved attitude making such comments as 'it was good to be able to reward positive behaviour to those who generally feel intimidated by the bad behaviour of the minority' and 'the effect changed depending on how strictly the exercise was applied – very effective at the beginning'. These comments would suggest a more difficult class to teach than is indicated in the old report. This does not mean that the teachers were deliberately misrepresenting what happens in their classrooms, it may be that the sheet did control the whole class for 26 out of 28 lessons. It could also be the case, though, and much more worryingly, that to be perhaps the only teacher on that sheet who appears to 'not cope' is far too anxiety-laden to contemplate. The old adage that a teacher's report says more about him than about the pupil is a concept that can freeze a teacher's willingness to give his professional judgement. That attitude and the isolation of teachers makes it difficult for them to say with confidence 'If this class is difficult for me they are difficult for anyone who is attempting to teach them appropriately rather than simply police them'. It can be seen that this aspect is potentially a key factor in behavioural and academic difficulties in schools, if classes can continue in an inappropriate learning environment with the unwitting collusion of the teachers. During my day of observation a teacher who wrote 'I don't know whether it has any value since the class is well behaved anyway' had left the class unattended on two occasions and had many interruptions connected to senior management administration during the lesson. The class were meanwhile each engaged on identical work that some of them could not read. There was no differentation. Although they thumped each other and threw things round when 'alone', they did 'keep their heads down' when the teacher was present. He had written on the old style report 'No trouble for me'!

Question 4 asked if they would like to use the scheme with other classes – only two subject teachers said they would.

The last question asked whether involvement with the scheme had changed

- their teaching style;
- lesson content;
- attitude; relationship with the class;
- their opinion of the group's potential.

Two teachers felt it gave them more insight into individuals' behaviour and to positive aspects of the group; one said it had focused his attention on his lesson plans, and another felt the group's organisation had improved as more homework appeared to be done well and handed in on time. One felt her attitude and relationship with them had changed but declined to say how as there was 'not enough space'.

I will now look at the questionnaires filled in by the tutor set teacher which are quite different in style. It must be remembered that he asked the outreach team to work with his tutor set and was deeply committed to the improvement of their learning environment. He returned two questionnaires. I will look first at the one he filled in as the teacher for whom the outreach project was initiated and then at the one he completed as a subject teacher who took them for a weekly active tutorial session.

He wrote,

> 'I have gained enormously in my role as tutor – in knowing the pupils, how they behaved in lessons, and social factors in greater detail. As a scientist it makes it so much more quantitative than the vague qualitative descriptions of behaviour before.'

He felt able and inclined to continue or run such an intervention again as 'it seems to be in line with active tutorial aims about self-awareness etc.'

He felt he would like to improve the scheme by contracting a specific reward for a high score or maybe a significant improvement, and he particularly felt parent contact was relevant in this context. He felt this could play a key role for 'borderline pupils who can go one way or the other.' He felt this tutor set had a large proportion of these.

As a teacher who saw them once a week he felt that pupils who had variable behaviour tended to start behaving well in every lesson, he also felt there was increased individual and group awareness. Interestingly, he felt he had increased awareness of the attitudes of the staff they met during the week. He felt very strongly that he could use the scheme to the advantage of most of the classes he taught. He comments,

'Most pupils seem to desperately want a tick and so the percentage of the class who could go either way all decided to be good and positive, leaving a small minority who could then be dealt with much more easily, especially as the others all regarded them as being anti-social. This made it easier for me to put into style, content, approval etc., what I would like to, rather than having to bear in mind discipline considerations in this planning. I found the scheme startling in its impact.'

It is interesting to note that after an observation of this teacher, doing a science lesson on bubbles with a different Year 8 group one month before I began to work on this intervention with him, I wrote

'great fun, bubbles everywhere!! All questions are welcome, an anxious late boy receives positive attention to settle him; differentiated instructions and questions to answer are clearly written on the board, it is a peaceful room for work with interesting posters representing a wide range of science activities on the wall, around the room are many pieces of interesting looking 'Professor Brainstorm-type' apparatus. This is not just a lesson, it is an experience they will remember for a long time – particularly when one boy tried to blow the biggest bubble ever and everyone stopped to watch'

As a piece of outreach work with a teacher I feel that this type of intervention has an exciting level of potential. This study does highlight however that to change attitudes is a long and difficult task. I would have preferred the subject teachers to meet more often to discuss the theory behind the scheme and its development. Initially a slot for this was set up when the teachers were first asked about the class, but after the first session in which several maintained 'they were no trouble for them' one probationer was extremely upset at this and refused to come again and apart from three teachers who were interested in meeting again the others all claimed they did not need it.

Recording the strategy for the Code of Practice

Primary example of recording the agreed strategy for the Code of Practice

1. Class teacher to go on keeping weekly sheets
    (a) to monitor changes
    (b) to count number of 'goods'.
2. Class teacher to introduce a calming exercise to start 'bad' days better.
3. Class teacher to prepare folder of 'success level' work to begin 'on-task' extension from 5 to 10 minutes to steady 15 minutes.
4. Class teacher to arrange 'paired work' experiences two or three times a week to build peer group relationships.
5. SENCO and class teacher to call a meeting with parents and social worker to discuss his morning routine. Child Protection Issues not to be raised with parents.
6. Social worker to pursue Child Protection Issues, sexualised behaviour and physical neglect.
7. Meet to review progress in four weeks after meeting parents.
8. Attach photocopies of weekly sheets to Code of Practice records for evidence.
9. Attach minutes of meetings to records.

Secondary example of recording the agreed strategy for the Code of Practice

1. Tutor set teacher to go on a running behaviour project.
2. Tutor set teacher to offer de-rolling exercise for 'bad start' days.
3. Letter home worded by child to be sent as weekly target achieved.
4. Year head to be used as 'reward' for pep talk to recognise success.
5. SENCO to work with English teacher to increase 'on-task' concentration time.
6. Close liaison with social services.
7. Regular meetings with parents/carers.
8. Review in four weeks.
9. Attach photocopies of weekly sheets for evidence.
10. Attach minutes of all meetings to Code of Practice records.

Step 4

Carrying out the Intervention

- Maintain the amount of attention for wanted behaviour the child has been negatively demanding.
- During this intervention normal school rules apply. Activities by the child which would normally incur sanctions should still do so.
- If you get a good idea to add something to the plan on the way through, that helps the child – do it.
- If the child seems disinterested in the reward he chose himself, don't change anything. He chose it, he wants it – he's probably insecure either that he can earn it or that you will keep your word.
- Do not discuss bad behaviour at all with the child or in his hearing. If you are also the teacher who delivers the school rule sanctions do so confidently, separating this in your mind from the programme. The programme is long term.
- Consult with a colleague if things happen that make you unsure of how to respond.
- Concentrate on good behaviour.
- Stick with the plan for the six weeks.
- Do not despair if the old behaviour is seen again. Is there a wider gap between occurrences, is it less intense?
- Remember that it took the child some years to get into this pattern, and it will take some time to change.
- Keep accurate weekly sheets, as they will help you to evaluate after six weeks. They are also your records for the Code of Practice.
- Sometimes children get worse before they get better. Don't change anything. Concentrate on good behaviour.
- When stuck, focus on something positive. Be scrupulously fair.
- Include staff, head teacher and/or parents in the praising if there is progress.
- Record the intervention on the weekly sheets. Attach photocopies to records.
- Photocopy sheets daily if necessary for the disorganised child who loses the sheet. He will get better at looking after it.
- Don't be tempted to forget about the programme if the child improves. His improvement means that what you are doing in working. So do not stop!

A selection of problems which might arise and ways forward if they do

Evaluating Success and Re-defining Remaining Difficulties

A range of possible outcomes and ways forward

This is one of the most important phases of an intervention of this kind. Review the six weekly sheets, preferably with a colleague or your SENCO. Has the original problem changed? In what way? *Using the Step 2 list, define the new problem as you did before.* Some questions to ask to evaluate your plan:

1. Have the weekly 'goods' increased?

2. If not, has the intensity of the behaviour reduced?

3. Has the intended strategy been in place exactly as planned?

4. Have all adults provided the promised rewards immediately and every time they were earned, as agreed with the child?

5. Have you added anything to the plan as you went along that helped or made administration easier?

6. Does the child seem disinterested in the reward he chose?

7. Have unexpected things happened? Are these good outcomes? Have unexpected things made progress more difficult?

8. Are adults hindering the progress of the plan? Are these parents or colleagues?

9. Does the child have insight to the remaining problem?

10. How does the child feel about how he's getting on?

11. Have his carers been consistently interested and supportive over the six weeks? How does this affect your future planning?

12. How do you feel about the plan?

13. Record your evaluation.

Examples of recording for the Code of Practice of the evaluation and re-defining the remaining problem

Secondary example
- Michael is still increasing the number of 'good' sessions on the programme, currently scoring between 31 and 35 'goods' out of 40. The 'de-role' exercise has been used by him to good effect.
- Michael has increased his concentration in class when required to be on-task.
- Letter home is valued by Michael.
- Year head being used as a reward has been very successful.
- Michael has made a friend.

Re-defining the remaining problem
- Occasional aggressive outbursts still occur.
- Parental support for letters and liaison meetings has been inconsistent.
- Still appears very vulnerable.
- Michael has had some out-of-school involvement with the police in recent weeks.

Primary example
- Pattern still persists that Darren is calmer after weekends with his natural father. He becomes extremely agitated before and after weekends. Calming exercise has helped but the level of distress is extreme.
- Has increased 'on-task' concentration time to consistent 10 minutes, sometimes achieving 15–20 minutes.
- Good relationship-building with classroom teacher.
- Pair work has resulted in some joint play in playground.
- Liaison with social worker has been regular.
- Darren has completed his first line of writing.
- Responds well to one-to-one support from classroom assistant when available.

Redefining the remaining problem
- There are still concerns regarding Child Protection Issues.
- Darren still arrives soiled, late and upset.
- Darren still appears to be under-achieving to a marked degree. See Individual Education Programme. Attached academic records.

Step 6

Planning the New Strategy

*1. Progress – only
slight alterations
needed*

- If the 'goods' are increased even by small amounts and/or the intensity has reduced even slightly, keep the existing plan in place for a further six weeks and evaluate again.
- It seems that what you are doing is working – remember that the child has been getting the way he is for years and six weeks is not long to get new behaviour established. Do not ease off.
- Make sure the amount of attention the child was getting negatively is maintained when his behaviour is good. Target him for appropriate positive feedback. Remember how much attention he got before. Don't let the rewards be forgotten.
- You may feel you want to adjust his education programme to the new situation. He may be getting more done or may have made progress and need slightly more challenge. Do this gradually. Keep a high success level.
- If he has been calmer you may feel you have a clearer picture of his learning or social needs and can enrich the plan with a response to these.
- If he is even slightly more predictable you may feel there is a suitable peer in the class to start pairing him up with. See Strategy III.
- Congratulate yourself!

2. No progress

No progress at all is very unusual.
  (a) Any progress – more good 'sessions'
                    – slight reduction in intensity
                    – even slightly lower frequency of negative incidents
                    – improvement in peer relations
means the programme is working, albeit slowly.
    Discuss the sheets you have collected with an honest colleague. Do they agree there has been *no* progress?
    Work through the questions at the beginning of Step 5 with that colleague.

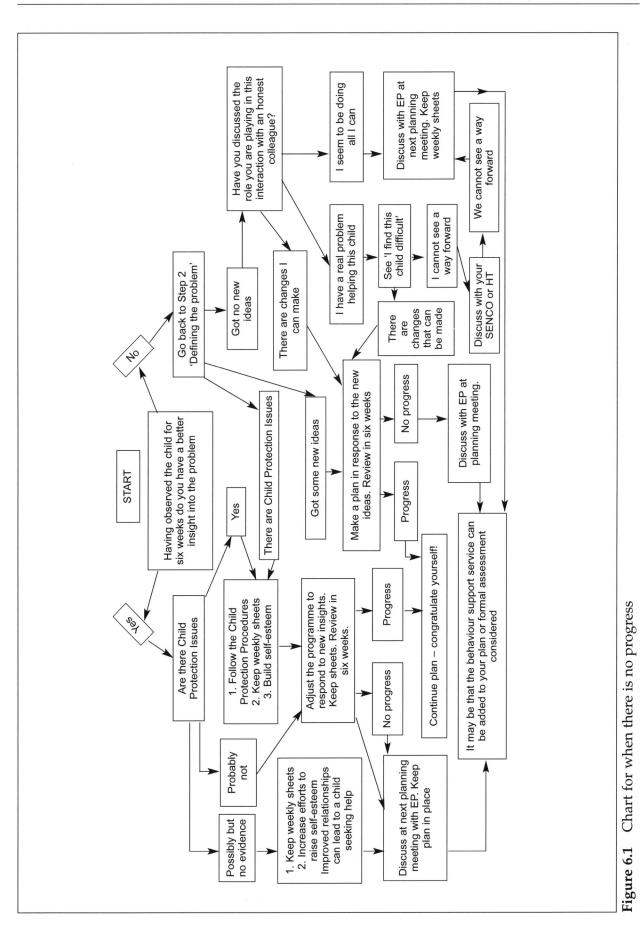

Figure 6.1 Chart for when there is no progress

It may be that you are playing a role in the programme unwittingly which is undermining its success.

Work through the 'I find this child difficult' section with your colleague. Pick out which of the 13 aspects of a teacher–pupil relationship may be the problem.

The following section contains strategies for teachers to help them overcome each of these difficulties. These strategies come under five main headings.

- Classroom atmosphere
- Classroom rules
- Being drawn into dysfunctional behaviour patterns
- Classroom organisation
- Personal difficulties

(b) It may be that entrenched difficulties within the child's family and a sustained series of traumatic events are making it impossible for the child to feel safe and relaxed. If there are Child Protection Issues follow the Child Protection Procedures.

(c) A 'review-of-progress' meeting with all the significant adults in the child's life can be a useful catalyst for change. If other agencies are involved with this child it is crucial that they coordinate their input. Parents, social services, health and education can report on the progress of their work with the child.

Next, each agency can agree what they are individually going to do to support this child before a follow-up meeting date agreed at the meeting.

(d) It may be that there is evidence that elements of the programme could be more successful but there is an issue of provision available at the School Action level. School will need to decide if a request for School Action Plus is appropriate.

Example of new strategy for secondary pupils

- Maintain existing programme and letters home. Keep weekly sheets as records.
- Include him in weekly group of peers talking about increasing their 'goods'.
- Explore local ways of getting him some one-to-one counselling. It may be necessary to access behavioural support services. A specific brief can now be given to such a service to enable them to add to the existing programme in a useful way.

Example of new strategy for primary pupils

- Maintain existing programme. Keep weekly sheets as records.
- Keep class work at success level.
- Close liaison with Social Services increased to weekly phone call to review.
- Monthly all-parties review meetings, including mother.
- Give attention to any child he hurts and not to him at the time of the incident.
- Nurture self-esteem in a structured, recorded programme.

This section can be used individually or by a year head or subject head in professional development sessions with other teachers.

1. Do you deliver praise with a negative sting in the tail? 'Well done Johnny – and about time too'.
2. Do you nag? 'How many times do I have to tell you?' 'You'll be the death of me'. 'I'll swing for you'. 'Don't you ever listen?'
3. Do you 'shout' – Is your 'whole-class' voice a high-pitched scream?
4. Do you use phrases you wouldn't use to adults at work? For example, 'You stupid boy', 'Get out of my room', 'Where do you think the pencils are?', 'You shut it'.
5. Do you let children tell you tales about this child? 'Mi-iss, Michael's sharpening his pencil again'.
6. Do you accept behaviour from other class members you won't accept from him? For example, two quiet-voiced girls talking while they are working – but he gets told off if he talks.
7. Do you give him ideas, 'Now I'm just going to the Head's room. Michael, I don't want to come back and find you on the window sill.'
8. Do you remember the difficulties in his life and try not to make it any worse for him?
9. Have you convinced him you want to help him?
10. Does your style mirror the difficulties he has at home? Discuss this with an honest colleague.
11. Do you feel this child especially affects you badly? Do you know why?
12. Are you less proactive just now in terms of classroom organisation and teaching plans than you know you should be? Does his low tolerance level show this up?
13. Are you currently very distracted yourself with a personal difficulty or poor health that makes the situation more difficult to deal with?

'I find this child difficult'. Aspects of the teacher–pupil relationship that can hinder progress

Strategies for teachers to help themselves

Points 1–4 Classroom atmosphere

You can have a visually wonderful classroom with interesting work for all, but if the atmosphere is negative you undo all your good work. One negative or verbally abusive lesson in a week can create an enormous amount of unnecessary extra work for yourself and your colleagues. Try tape recording yourself while teaching. Listen to it in private!

(a) To keep self-esteem of children level, aim for five positive remarks to one negative. To raise self-esteem you need to nearly double that. Are you making ten positive remarks to one negative?

(b) Are you interrupting concentration by loud whole-class instructions suddenly and unpredictably: can organisation reduce this?

(c) Your voice is an important part of your professional repertoire. Can you develop an effective tone and positive ways of achieving your aims?

(d) Could *you* concentrate in the atmosphere you are creating?

(e) Have you tried peaceful music playing quietly while children arrive at your lesson or during creative sessions? How did it affect the atmosphere?

(f) If there are times in the classroom when you want silent working have you discussed and established a rule that is respected and gets the result you want? Do you need to re-establish this rule with your class? Do you need ideas from a colleague whom you trust who seems to achieve this?

(g) Do classes come regularly from one colleague upset, disorientated or rowdy? Has anything been done about it?

Points 5–7 Classroom rules

It may be that the difficult child can be like 'a canary in the mine' to measure the effectiveness of your rules. When he is contained and secure so is everyone else.

(a) Do you re-establish the rules regularly with new groups?

(b) Do children know how to get it right for you?

(c) Which rule is hardest for you to enforce – Why? What can you do about that?

Points 8–9 Are teachers getting drawn into dysfunctional patterns of behaviour?

Children who have learnt unskilful ways of expressing their emotions, or who need more attention than good behaviour generally gets, are difficult to relate to. The following responses are uncomfortable but quite common. It can be helpful to discuss this with subject teachers.

- They are hard to 'read' and so hard to understand or predict.
- Their neediness can tap into our needs.
- They can project their anger on to us and we play the other half when we could break the cycle instead.
- The sadness and hardship in their lives can shock us and make us unwittingly reject them.
- We can reciprocate by having sadness and hardship of our own triggered into an uncomfortable position in our minds.
- They can remind us uncomfortably of a difficult sibling of our own or a person we have found difficult.
- We can unwittingly use them as scapegoats for our own frustrations.
- They can make us feel powerless and we can show our resistance by rejecting them.
- We can use them unwittingly as a model for the class of what not to be. If this becomes an essential part of the group dynamic, everyone needs him to stay the same and not get better.
- If the child is to be changed it is essential for the adult to maintain a consistent style of skilful emotional expression and situation appropriate behaviour. This is not easy and needs both management and peer support. Teacher behaviour works as a model for all the children in the group and should make sure everyone is treated well. The relationship of teacher to child is a professional one.

Enlist the help you need to support you and congratulate yourself for the resulting success.

Point 10 Your style mirrors his difficulties at home
This is difficult to identify yourself. You may need a colleague's help. See Section VII, 4 (p. 27).

If, for instance, you raise your voice a lot, most children will cope, understanding the context. However, the child that is shouted at abusively at home may not be able to do that. You may notice a deterioration on his weekly sheets in lessons where this happens. Similarly, if a child's home circumstances involve a high level of unpredictable changes, he may react more strongly to this in your teaching style than other children.

Being aware of this kind of effect, being flexible in your style to accommodate differences, will help.

Points 11–12 Classroom organisation
There is nothing as good as a child with a low tolerance level for exposing the weaknesses that creep into classroom organisation. See it as a positive motivator and make the necessary changes. They will benefit everyone. Congratulate yourself on the resulting improvement!

Point 13 Personal difficulties

Teaching is in the top 2 per cent of stressful jobs. It is physically and emotionally draining. You work in an exposed situation in front of 'clients' all day and are physically restricted to the room most of the day. You cannot even take a holiday when you need it, if that happens to be in the middle of the term. When you are on holiday, resorts are full of children!

Most other jobs have access to telephones, toilets and peace and quiet within reason at the free choice of the adults. Most adults have flexible lunch hours and can make a drink when they need to during the day. Schools are also not the most comfortable work environments and are often draughty, poorly heated or too hot.

We know it can be wonderful fun and extremely rewarding but at times when personal difficulties are uppermost or you are in poor health it is an extremely difficult job to 'stay on top of'. If you lose a proactive approach, teaching becomes more difficult.

Strategies for looking after yourself

- Counselling can help by creating a regular slot in your week to off-load and to have the problem-solving support you need. It is important to look after yourself so that your mind is clear.
- Peer support is really important – everyone finds teaching stressful and sharing problems helps.
- Getting organised so that everything runs as smoothly as possible makes life easier.
- Preparing differentiated work well ahead for those children who will be disruptive helps. This means they are kept busy with a series of relevant tasks that are balanced well between success level, consolidation tasks and new learning experiences.
- If you need sick leave, take it without guilt, with your doctor's advice. It is better for the school's organisation if you and your doctor can calculate a block of time at the end of which you expect to be fully better. This means that a supply teacher can be given clear advice as to how long he will be with your class and you will be more likely to come back to a settled situation. Extending sick leave on a daily basis means a supply teacher can only organise for a day at a time. This also creates more administration as supply teachers have to be asked every day if they can stay or new ones found. Coming back before you are better means that you are likely to be off again, thus disrupting the class again.
- Make sure you have recreational activities outside of school that meet your social and emotional needs.

> **Keypoint** – Congratulate yourself on changes that improve things.

Appendix 1*

SCHOOL ACTION RECORD SHEET

Priority concern – emotional and behavioural difficulties

To be started at the first indication of difficulty.

Name of child   Home language
Address   Parents
                                           Class group   Year
D.o.b.   Age   Date first on register
Teacher

INITIAL OBSERVATIONS

2 weeks' observation using blank timetables.
Attach 2 weeks' timetable sheets of observation by class teacher.

DEFINITION OF PROBLEM – from attached sheets
Number of good sessions obtained in each week   Wk 1 =   /
(Give full total possible.)   Wk 2 =   /

Behaviour Difficulties

Academic Difficulties

* 0This form may be photocopied for use within the purchasing institution. It may also be downloaded from the publishers website www.fultonpublishers.co.uk

© Geraldine Mitchell (2001) *Practical Strategies for Individual Behaviour Difficulties*. London: David Fulton Publishers.   www.fultonpublishers.co.uk

**STRATEGY PLANNED – To be carried out for _____ weeks and reviewed.
Record using weekly sheets.**

Strategy for Behaviour Difficulties

Strategy for Academic Difficulties

EVALUATION OF INTERVENTION (Discuss with SENCO if appropriate)

(Attach _____ weeks of observation sheets.)

Number of good sessions obtained for each week of the intervention.

Wk 1__

Wk 2__

Wk 3__

Wk 4__

Wk 5__

Wk 6__

	Yes	No
Has the number of good sessions increased		
Have there been differences in what you have seen?		

Behaviour Difficulties

Academic Difficulties

DEFINITION OF THE REMAINING PROBLEM

Behaviour Difficulties

Academic Difficulties

'STRATEGY PLANNED' to continue cycle until the problem no longer exists.

Strategy for Behaviour Difficulties

Strategy for Academic Difficulties

Primary school example of recording

Example I

SCHOOL ACTION RECORD SHEET

Priority concern – emotional and behavioural difficulties

To be started at the first indication of difficulty.

Name of child   Home language

Address   Parents

                                              Class group   Year

D.o.b.   Age (YR 2)   Date first on register

Teacher

INITIAL OBSERVATIONS

2 weeks' observation using blank timetables.

Attach 2 weeks' timetable sheets of observation by class teacher. ✓✓

DEFINITION OF PROBLEM – from attached sheets

Number of good sessions obtained in each week	Wk 1 = ^{18}/30
(Give full total possible.)	Wk 2 = ^{20}/30

Behaviour Difficulties

- Gets on well with adults 1 to 1, but finds peer group difficult
- Gets into trouble regularly at dinner time play (3 x weekly)
- Evidence of physical neglect, is often quite outside broad average.
- Difficulties in peer group relationships can often be excessively aggressive.
- works well on structured tasks, finds creative tasks difficult

Academic Difficulties

(record I.E.P. as usual)

STRATEGY PLANNED – To be carried out for __6__ weeks and reviewed.
Record using weekly sheets.

Strategy for Behaviour Difficulties

Strategy I - c/t, senior management and dinner supervisor will coordinate dinner time strategy.

Strategy III - c/t will pair with appropriate pupil consistently for P.E, responsibilities, discussion tasks and tasks which require reciprocation. these may need differentiation.

Strategy VII 2. - c/t will follow an intensive programme of self-esteem enhancement.

Strategy X - c/t and senco to meet with parents to encourage them to raise his self esteem. Physical neglect will be addressed.

c/t will continue to keep the weekly sheets.

Strategy for Academic Difficulties

(record I.E.P. as usual)

EVALUATION OF INTERVENTION (Discuss with SENCO if appropriate)

(Attach __6__ weeks of observation sheets.

Number of good sessions obtained for each week of the intervention.

Wk 1 __19__

Wk 2 __23__

Wk 3 __27__ Half term

Wk 4 __16__

Wk 5 __25__

Wk 6 __27__

	Yes	No
Has the number of good sessions increased	✓	
Have there been differences in what you have seen?	✓	

Behaviour Difficulties

- Scored much less after the half term week.
- Lunchtime strategy worked well quite quickly, but needed to be re-introduced after ½ term when this area was more vulnerable again. Improvement was quicker this time.
- Still struggles with peer group - but has been seen playing with 'pair' in dinner time. This play has been successful.
- Has appeared a little calmer but further encouragement is needed on both physical neglect and self esteem at home.
- Self esteem programme at school seems to be giving him more confidence with open-ended tasks. (see sheets) but he is still vulnerable
- Aggression is less often (see sheets) but still occurs.

Academic Difficulties

(record I.E.P. as usual)
- Now that 'learning behaviour' is beginning to be established - work given needs to reflect his ability to do 10 mins independent work.

DEFINITION OF THE REMAINING PROBLEM

Behaviour Difficulties

- Deterioration in behaviour after time at home. Physical neglect and low self-esteem still evident.
- Continues to need differentiation to establish reciprocal peer group relationships. Particularly needs help to resolve differences.
- Gets upset less but finds it hard to calm himself when he does.

Academic Difficulties

(record I.E.P as usual)
- resists absorption in independent class work
- responds well to structure - appears to still 'fear' open-ended creative tasks.
- responds well to adult support but can be overly reliant on this

'STRATEGY PLANNED' to continue cycle until the problem no longer exists.

Strategy for Behaviour Difficulties

- Set up regular supportive meetings with parents. TO. 1. Feedback successes
  2. To discuss behaviour management at home
  3. To support parents in developing self-esteem enhancing ways.
(It may be necessary to suggest parent seeks some family support from Social Services.) meetings to be at beginning and end of each half-term with SENCO and c/t.
- Dinner time strategy to be used after holidays
- Self-esteem enhancement to continue and be extended to small
- 'Pair' work to continue and be extended to small regular groups. Help offered to resolve difficulties peace rules.
Strategy VIII - c/t will set up 'thinking chair.'
Review termly

Strategy for Academic Difficulties

(Record I.E.P as usual)

Strategy IX - c/t will provide folder for consolidation work for independence practise.

Strategy XI - c/t will differentiate creative tasks into more structured steps.

SENCO will direct appropriate funds to provide in class support to lead towards greater independence.

Review ½ termly.

Appendix 3

Secondary school example of recording

Example 2
SCHOOL ACTION RECORD SHEET
Priority concern – emotional and behavioural difficulties

To be started at the first indication of difficulty.

Name of child   Home language

Address   Parents

                               Class group   Year

D.o.b.   Age (YR 8)   Date first on register

Teacher

INITIAL OBSERVATIONS
2 weeks' observation using blank timetables.

Attach 2 weeks' timetable sheets of observation by class teacher. ✓✓

DEFINITION OF PROBLEM – from attached sheets

Number of good sessions obtained in each week   Wk 1 = $^9/40$

(Give full total possible.)   Wk 2 = $^{13}/40$

Behaviour Difficulties

- Copes reasonably well with playground but resists complying in the classroom.
- Gets on well with adults 1 to 1 but finds peer group friendships difficult.
- Certain days are more difficult than others from the start. On these days child arrives upset and late.
- Output of written work is drastically below broad average.
- A small insult sets off an over-reaction which often includes aggression.
- Finds it hard to return to a state of calm.
- There is deterioration after holidays.

Academic Difficulties

- Has missed initial screening assessments as he has just joined the school
- Appears to have gaps in his education.

STRATEGY PLANNED – To be carried out for __6__ weeks and reviewed.
Record using weekly sheets.

Strategy for Behaviour Difficulties

Strategy XIV - To be included in year heads positive reward project for 6-8 pupils This includes positive behaviour target setting programme across the curriculum and membership in weekly group. Targets to be easily obtainable at first.

Strategy VI - year head/tutor set teacher to set up appropriate routine for late mornings.

Strategy X - tutor/year head to meet with mother. As they are living in a refuge home visit not possible.

Strategy VIII - 'Calming down strategy' to be discussed in group session with year head and practised using own watch.

Strategy for Academic Difficulties

• Senco to carry out full assessment of academic achievement.
• The family have moved alot - Senco to trace missing records.
• Senco to advise subject teachers of differentiation necessary.
• Senco to direct School Action funding for in class support as appropriate.

EVALUATION OF INTERVENTION (Discuss with SENCO if appropriate)

(Attach __6__ weeks of observation sheets. ✓

Number of good sessions obtained for each week of the intervention.

Wk 1 __17__ – target was 10 letter home
Wk 2 __20__ – " " 11 " "
Wk 3 __16__ – " " 12 " " (recieved a 1 day exclusion for aggression)
Wk 4 __24__ – " " 13 " "
Wk 5 __28__ – " " 17 " "
Wk 6 __36__ – " " 20 " "

	Yes	No
Has the number of good sessions increased	✓	
Have there been differences in what you have seen?	✓	

Behaviour Difficulties

- Is relating well to year head + tutor. Staff across the curriculum are noticing change for the better. Still finds independent work difficult.
- WK 3 contained an excessive over reaction to a minor insult from a peer. An exclusion resulted. Programme rules continued. Happens less often but is still part of the problem.
- letter home to his brother is a valued reward.
- meeting with mother useful. Mum is very caring but exhausted.
- Mondays are usually the worst day. It also seems the volatile relationship the father has with the family leaves the boy feeling responsible for their safety – hence the upset mornings.
- Some specific lessons remain difficult to get 'goods' in.
- Is contributing well in the 'group' and has made a friend in it.
- Has been trying to practise 'calming strategy'. This has been occasionally successful.

Academic Difficulties

- Testing shows him to be far behind his peers. This is most markedly in his basic numeracy and literacy skills. However the gaps in education affect his performance in all areas of the curriculum.
- It appears from his records and the information the SENCO has discovered from previous schools, there have been many moves of school and addresses throughout his childhood and particularly when he was very young. Social services have been involved throughout.

DEFINITION OF THE REMAINING PROBLEM

Behaviour Difficulties

- Still arrives late and upset on occasions
- Can still react inappropriately aggressively to minor insults.
- Still finds some lessons difficult, particularly maths, french and occasionally science - depending which teacher takes it.
- Always remembers when the group is and reminds others. Has said he would attend it after school. Encourages others in the group to express their feelings.

Academic Difficulties

- Pupil appears to be markedly underachieving in all areas of the curriculum.
- Gaps exist in all areas of his learning.
- However newly taught material is well understood and estimates of outcome in science are well based.

'STRATEGY PLANNED' to continue cycle until the problem no longer exists.

Strategy for Behaviour Difficulties

- Continue programme as it is for a further 6 weeks. i.e. Group/positive reward programme/lateness strategy/liaison with mother
- Include more focus on 'anger management' in "group" conversations of year heads project.

- Continue to keep the record sheets from the positive reward programme to monitor progress & reward.

- REVIEW in 6 weeks.

Strategy for Academic Difficulties

- Include in intensive small group to 'boost' basic skills.
- target difficult lessons for classroom support
- Introduce Strategy $\overline{IX}$ in English + Maths lessons for him and possible small group who find absorption in task difficult.

(reward I.E.P. as usual)

Bibliography

Ainscow, M. and Muncey, J. (1989) *Meeting Individual Needs in the Primary School.* London: David Fulton Publishers.

Anderson, L. S. and Limoncelli, R. J. (1982) 'Meeting the needs of high risk, difficult to teach students: creative education approaches', *The School Counsellor* **29**(6) May.

Ball, S. J. and Goodson, A. (1985) *Teacher' Lives and Careers.* London: Falmer Press.

Bandura, A. and Walters, R. H. (1959) *Adolescent Aggression.* New York: Ronald Press.

Bannister, D. and Fransella, F. (1971) *Inquiring Man: The Theory of Personal Construct.* London: Penguin Books.

Barrett, M. and Varma, Ved (1996) *Educational Therapy in Clinic and Classroom.* London: Whurr Publishers.

Bassey, M. 'Does action research require sophisticated research methods', in Hustler, D., Cassidy, T., Clift, T. (eds) *Action Research in Classrooms and Schools.* London: Allen & Unwin Publishers.

Bell, J. and Harrison, B. T. (1995) *Vision and Values in Managing Education.* London: David Fulton Publishers.

Best, R. *et al.* (1995) *Pastoral Care and Personal and Social Education.* London: Cassell.

Blum, M. L. and Naylor, V. C. (1968) *Industrial Psychology.* London: Harper Row.

Booth, T. and Potts, P. (1983) *Integrating Special Education.* Oxford: Blackwell Publishers.

Brotherton, C. (1988) 'Technological change and innovation –setting the agenda for occupational psychology', *Journal of Occupational Psychology* **61**, 1–5.

DES (1978) Warnock Report. *'Special Educational Needs'.* London: HMSO.

DES (1987) *Good Behaviour and Discipline in Schools.* London: HMSO.

Docket, J. G., Fraser, B. J. and Fischer, D. L. (1989) 'Differences in the social work environment of different types of schools', *Journal of Research in Childhood Education* **14**(1), 5–16.

Dyke, S. (1985) 'Getting better makes it worse', *Maladjustment and Therapeutic Education,* **3**(3).

Elliott, J. and Adelmann, C. (1977) *Ford Teaching Project.* Cambridge: Cambridge Institute of Education.

Ellis, S. (1985) 'The work of the DO5 Schools Support Team', *Maladjustment and Therapeutic Education,* **3**(2).

Elton, Lord. (1989) *Discipline in Schools.* London: Department of Education and Science.

Erikson, E. (1968) Identity, Youth and Crisis. London: Faber & Faber.

Farrington D. P. (1978) 'The family background of aggressive youths', in Herson, L.A., Berger, M., Sheffer, D. (eds) *Aggression and Anti-Social Behaviour in Childhood and Adolescence.* London: Pergamon Press.

Fischer, Kurt W. (1990) 'How emotions develop and how they organise development', *Cognition and Emotion,* **4**(2), 81–127.

Foulkes, S. H. Anthony, E. J. (1957) *Group Therapy.* London: Pelican.

Fraser, B. J. (1987) 'Use of classroom environment assessments in school psychology', *School Psychology International* **8**, 205–219.

Gale, A. (1991) 'The School as organisation: new roles for psychologists in education', *Psychology in Practice,* **7**(2), 67–73.

Gray, J. and Wilcox, W. (1995) *Good School, Bad School.* Milton Keynes: Open University Press.

Hackett, R. (1989) 'Work attitudes and employee absenteeism: a synthesis of the literature', *Journal of Occupational Psychology,* **62**(3) 235–248.

Hanko, G. (1985) *Special Needs in the Ordinary Classroom.* London: Blackwell Publishers.

Hargreaves, D. H. (1975) *Social Relations in the Secondary School.* London: Routledge & Kegan Paul.

Hegarty, S. and Pocklington, K. (1981) *Educating Pupils with Special Needs in the Ordinary School.* London: NFER-Nelson.

HMSO (1993) *Code of Practice on the Identification and Assessment of Special Educational Needs.* London: HMSO.

HMSO (1993) *Education Act.* London: HMSO.

HMSO (2000) *Code of Practice on the Identification and Assessment of Special Educational Needs* (consultation document). London: HMSO.

Hoghughi, M. (1988) *Treating Problem Children.* London: Sage Publications.

Jankowitz, D. (1987) 'Whatever became of George Kelly?' *American Psychologist,* **May**, 481–87.

Kelly, G. (1955) *The Psychology of Personal Constructs.* New York: W. W. Norton.

Lawrence, D. (1987) *Enhancing Self Esteem in the Classroom.* London: Paul Chapman Publishing.

Lewis, D. (1981) *You Can Teach Your Child Intelligence.* London: Sphere.

Malatesta, C. Z. *et al.* (1989) 'The development of emotional expression during the first two years of life', *Monograph of the Society for Research of Child Development* Serial No. 219, **54** Nos 1–2.

McCormick, E. J. and Ugen, D. R. (1987) *Industrial and Organisational Psychology.* London: Allen & Unwin Publishers.

Merrit, F. and Wheldall, K. (1986) 'Training teachers to use the behavioural approach to classroom management', in *The Behaviourist in the Classroom.* London: Allen & Unwin Publishers.

Moos, R. H. (1986) *Work Environment Scale.* Oxford: Oxford University Press.

Nicholls, T. (1986) *The British Worker: A New Look at Workers and Productivity in Manufacturing.* London: Routledge & Kegan Paul.

Perinpanayagam, K. S. (1987) 'Organisation and management of an in-patient treatment unit for adolescents', *Journal of Adolescents,* **10**, 133–148.

Porras, J. I. and Silvers, R. C. (1991) 'Organisation development and transformation', *Annual Review Psychology,* **42**, 51–78.

Ribeaux, P. and Poppleton, S. E. (1989) *Psychology and Work.* London: Macmillan Publishers.

Rutter, M. (1979) *Fifteen Thousand Hours: Secondary Schools and their Effects on Children.* Cambridge, Mass.: Harvard University Press.

Rutter, M. (1985) 'Family and school influences on behaviour development', *Journal of Psychology and Psychiatry,* **26**(3), 349–67.

Springer, Sally P. (1989) *Right Brain, Left Brain,* 3rd. edn. Basingstoke: W. H. Freeman.

Strongman, K. T. (1987) *The Psychology of Emotions,* 3rd edn. Chichester: John Wiley & Sons.

Tanzer, N. K. (1990) 'A dual-level approach to assessing social climates as perceived by students, teachers and parents', *The German Journal of Psychology,* **14**(1), 13–20.

Taylor, D. and Dowling, E. (1986) 'The clinic goes to school: setting up an outreach service', *Maladjustment and Therapeutic Education,* **4**(2), 12–18.

Thomas, D. (1985) 'The dynamics of teacher opposition to integration', *Remedial Education,* **20**(2), 53–7.

Tindal, G., Shinn, N. R., Rodden-Nord, K. (1990) 'Contextually based school consultation: influential variables', *Exceptional Children,* **56**(4), 324–36.

Woods, P. (1980) *Teachers Strategies.* London: Croom Helm.

Index